Robert F. Allen, Ph.D. is president of the Human Resources Institute in Morristown, New Jersey. As a consultant to corporations, communities, hospitals and government agencies, he has been responsible for developing and implementing hundreds of successful organizational and community change programs based on the Normative Systems change process. He is professor emeritus of psychology and policy sciences at Kean College of New Jersey, and has published more than 200 books, articles, and films on organizational and community change.

Charlotte Kraft, prior to her death in 1985, was involved in the design of many of HRI's programs and educational, community, and organizational change projects. She was a teacher, freelance writer, playwright, writing consultant, and an editor for the Human Resources Institute.

Judd Allen received his Ph.D. in Community Psychology from New York University. He is currently Executive Director of the Institute for Cultural Analysis and Change, a Vice President of the Human Resources Institute, and a faculty member at Cornell University Medical College. Dr. Allen served as a Senior Research Analyst at Memorial Sloan-Kettering Cancer Center. He is a published poet, a member of the editorial board of the American Journal of Health Promotion, and has written extensively on health promotion and organization development in community and business settings.

Barry Certner is the Executive Vice President of the Human Resources Institute. He received his Ph.D. in Clinical and Community Psychology and serves as a consultant to major corporations and communities. Dr. Certner has served as the Director of Programs and Laboratories at the National Training Institute for Applied Behavioral Science (NTL Institute) and as director of the National Sex Roles Institute sponsored by the Psychiatric Institute Foundation. He has been responsible for the development of HRI's pioneering culture-based programs in the field of alcohol and drug abuse.

P9-DEI-330

THE
ORGANIZATIONAL
UNCONSCIOUS

*How to Create the Corporate Culture
You Want and Need*

Human Resources Institute
115 Dunder Rd Burlington, VT
05401 (802) 862-8855
www.healthyculture.com

Human Resources Institute
Tempe Wick Road, Morristown, NJ 07960

Library of Congress Cataloging in Publication Data

Allen, Robert Francis (date).
   The organizational unconscious.

   Bibliography: p.
   Includes index.
   1. Organization.   2. Management.   I. Kraft, Charlotte.
II. Title.
HD31. A416 1982   658.4'06   82-7648
ISBN 0-941703-00-2   AACR2

This HRI book can be made available to businesses and organizations
at a special discount when ordered in large quantities.
For more information, contact: Human Resources Institute,
Tempe Wick Road, Morristown, New Jersey 07960

1 2 3 4 5 6 7 8 9 10

ISBN 0-941703-00-2

Editorial/production supervision by Rita Young
Cover design by Hal Siegel

Contents

Preface

All of us who have been associated with organizations recognize that massive amounts of time and energy are invested in their care and nurture. We also recognize how immensely important it is for us that our organizations succeed. Many hours, days, weeks, months, and even years are devoted to finding the best ways of making this happen. Yet, despite prodigious efforts, many of our organizations fall far short of their goals and pay the price in frustration, disappointment, and unsatisfactory levels of achievement.

Too often the struggle of a leader to build and maintain an effective organization resembles the effort of a strong swimmer endeavoring to swim upstream against the force of a rapidly flowing river. Despite heroic efforts, the swimmer is either swept into the current or back to land, exhausted. The swimmer may achieve some headway through strong beginning efforts, but in the final analysis, the river has its way.

As we go about our work in organizations, currents beneath the surface influence our direction, operating without our knowledge and frustrating our best efforts. To use a Freudian analogy, it is as if an unconscious level of activity blocks the achievement of our conscious goals.

This book proposes that the most viable way to assure the success and well-being of organizations is to recognize these strong undercurrents and to deal with them in a systematic, humanistic way. The first step is to recognize that an organization is made up of cultural norms that can be maintained or changed at the discretion of its members. These cultural expectations form underlying patterns that, like the individual's subconscious, largely determine whether the organization's goals will be achieved.

This book is intended to offer business, organizational, and community leaders a planned, systematic, generic process that uses cultural analysis as a way of gaining greater insight into the problems of organizations, and cultural change as a way of improving the quality of organizational life.

Part I of the book presents the concept of the organizational unconscious together with a four-stage model for bringing about cultural change. Part II focuses on the cultural role supportive environments play in implementing and maintaining change. Part III shows how the cultural change process can be applied to various organizational problems.

The change process suggested here proposes a greater participative dimension, involving people from all levels of an organization in the analysis of problems, setting goals, modification of behavior, and evaluation of results. Thus "ownership" of a change project is widespread among all those who will be affected by it.

The cultural approach to change helps to sustain the mutually agreed upon changes that are sought, so that they survive the switching of chiefs, the replacement of one managerial program by another, and the encroachments and fluctuations of the outer environment.

In planning and writing this book we have been influenced by hundreds of prior studies. We are also indebted to the thousands of people who have taken part in the culture change programs that we have been involved with. It would be impossible to name them all, but we wish to extend a special thanks to Harry Dubin and Saul Pilnick, whose early collaborative efforts at Scientific Resources, Inc., provided some of the seminal ideas that led to the concepts described in the book; to Doris Ballantyne for her skills, efficiency, and good humor in typing the manuscript; and to Elaine, Judd, and Peter Allen for their personal support.

From the many others who provided encouragement we particularly want to thank Rick Bellingham, Allen Bildner, Barry Certner, George Dann, Jack Dreyer, Annette and Roger Kraft, Moe Liss, Stephanie and Ralph Litwin, Mary Sochet, Walter Stein, Jim Vaughan, and Andy Workum.

Acknowledgments

Robert F. Allen, "The Ik in the Office," *Organizational Dynamics*, 8, no. 3 (Winter 1980), 129, 134, and 136–37. Excerpted by permission of the publisher. Copyright © 1980 by AMACOM, a division of the American Management Associations. All rights reserved.

Robert F. Allen, "When Are Results Not Results," (Selected Paper no. 7, March 1979), 21–25. Organization Development Division (American Society of Training and Development). Reprinted by permission of the publisher.

Robert F. Allen and Charlotte Kraft, "From Burn-out to Turn-on: Improving the Quality of Hospital Work Life, *Hospital Forum* (Journal of the Association of Western Hospitals) May–June 1981, pp. 174-84. Reprinted by permission of the publisher.

Robert F. Allen and Charlotte Kraft, "You Can Mobilize Your Community Toward Health," *Perspective*, 6, no. 2 and no. 4, 1980. Reprinted with permission from *Perspective* (Journal of Professional YMCA Directors in the United States). Copyright Spring-Summer 1980.

Robert F. Allen and Michael Higgins, "The Absenteeism Culture: Becoming Attendance Oriented," *Personnel*, January 1979, pp. 155–73. Reprinted by permission of the publisher, from *Personnel*. Copyright © 1979 by AMACOM, a division of the American Management Associations. All rights reserved.

Excerpt from "Changing the Corporate Culture," by Robert F. Allen and Stanley Silverzweig, *Sloan Management Review*, 17, no. 3, pp. 141–54, reprinted by permission of the publisher. Copyright © 1976 by the Sloan Management Review Association. All rights reserved.

Chris Argyris, "Double Loop Learning in Organizations," *Harvard Business Review* (September-October 1977). Excerpt reprinted by permission of the Harvard Business Review. Copyright © 1977 by the President and Fellows of Harvard College. All rights reserved.

Warren Bennis, *Organizational Development: Its Nature, Origin, and Prospects* (Reading, Mass.: Addison-Wesley, 1969), p. 75. © 1969, by Addison-Wesley. Excerpt reprinted by permission of the publisher.

Jay Galbraith, *Designing Complex Organizations* (Reading, Mass.: Addison-Wesley, 1973) p. 4. © 1973, by Addison-Wesley. Reprinted with permission of the publisher.

Christopher Lasch, *The Culture of Narcissism* (New York: W.W. Norton, 1979), p. 122. Reprinted with permission of the publisher.

E.F. Schumacher, Good Work (New York: Harper & Row, 1979) p. 76. Reprinted with permission of Harper & Row.

Daniel Yankelovich, Florence Skelly, and Arthur White, "Family Health in an Era of Stress," as reported in the *New York Times*, April 26, 1979. © 1979 by The New York Times Company. Reprinted by permission.

I

THE ORGANIZATIONAL UNCONSCIOUS

chapter one

Discovering Your Organization's Unconscious

Once upon a time there was a large corporation that instituted an exciting, company-wide organization development (OD) effort. The fairy godmothers came in with their magic OD wands, and a great transformation seemed to take place. Enthusiastic managers installed change programs and introduced them to hundreds of employees through a series of meetings and task force activities. There was a sense of shared commitment, and many people contributed ideas for improvements. Productivity soared, and morale surveys were positive. There was a new spirit in the company, reaching from the Chief Executive Officer (CEO) to the newest hourly employees.... And they all lived happily thereafter, until—until the fairy godmothers pulled out and went to wave their magic wands in other companies. The corporation continued to do well for a while, but then bottom-line figures began to slip a little, and the morale survey showed a downward trend. There were rumblings beneath the surface, and the old ways of doing things began to creep back in. In five years the corporation was back operating in much the same old way. There was some talk about calling the OD specialists back, but the prevailing attitude was, "We tried it and it didn't seem to work, so why try again?"

   This sad and puzzling fairy tale has been played out with many variations in our offices, corporate halls, factories, schools, communities, and in our public and private institutions. Why don't the changes we make last? Why can't we have the kind of organizations we really want? Over and over again improvement efforts are thwarted by invisible, unacknowledged forces. It is as if each organization were in reality two organizations—one visible, articulated, expressed in stated goals, policy statements, and procedural manuals; the other invisible, lying quietly under the surface, but actually determining what will happen in the long run. This unseen but powerful force might be called the *organizational unconscious*.

The idea of an individual unconscious has been with us since Sigmund Freud contributed his systematic analysis of unseen personal forces that work beneath the surface of our awareness, determining so much of our individual behavior. In dealing with organizations, we find it useful to envision another form of unconscious, one that exerts a powerful influence on group behavior. As we conceptualize it, the organizational unconscious represents those patterns of social behavior and normative expectations that become characteristic of an organization's functioning, without its members consciously choosing them. These norms determine much of what people in organizations do, and even when the patterns of behavior have outlived their usefulness, people act as if they were the only ones that could possibly exist under the circumstances. "It's just the way things are around here."

We often see what happens when the organizational unconscious is not understood and dealt with. When a program is imposed upon an organization without dealing with its "unconscious," at first the change may appear to succeed, but gradually unseen forces take over until finally the change is no longer visible. The organization, like a giant, soft, resilient pillow, accepts the changes laid upon it, then gradually puffs out again as if nothing had happened. Results are only temporary—they cannot be permanent results until the organizational unconscious is dealt with effectively and the "soft pillow" of the organization is remolded into a shape that will support the desired innovations.

Unfortunately, most efforts at change, even when we label them as "cooperation" or "teamwork" or "total organizational effort," fall far short of treating the unconscious forces and therefore are destined to be short-lived. An organization can take a lot of surface change, and can take it on quickly, but it can just as quickly absorb that change and return to its original state or one that is even worse.

What we think of as "results" often turns out to be not results at all, but merely temporary change. We see this happen with zero-base budgeting, management-by-objectives, litter clean-up campaigns, the crackdown on nursing home and safety violations, to name a few. Many, many programs achieve what their perpetrators and even their critics call results, which in the long run are not results at all—and may even end up creating more problems than they solve by fostering frustration and a sense of helplessness.

Once we recognize that this invisible, powerful force exists, our change efforts will be widely affected. Then we will see that it is not enough to say at the end of a "turning-on" weekend at a conference center in the Poconos, "Okay, now go back to the home office and do it." There has to be a means to install new behavior so that it becomes part of the fabric of the organization. Similarly, in a community there has to be a way to transform community-wide goals into neighborhood action, and in a school there has to be a way to get the good things planned in committee meetings off the paper and into the daily norms of the classroom.

SEEING YOUR ORGANIZATION AS A CULTURE

The primary premise of this book is that the way to deal with the organizational unconscious—to change its patterns and make the new ways stick—lies in treating the organization as a culture. To become masters of our work environments, we need first to see the cultural aspect very clearly.

Seeing the organization as a culture has wide ramifications, for it means shedding a humanistic light upon it, encouraging us to treat its members not as roles but as full human beings. The approach can be contrasted with a narrower type of "systems approach" or "systems analysis process," which starts with a model of the organization as a mechanical system and proceeds to make stepwise analyses and development programs. In a cultural approach, people are treated as multidimensional persons rather than as component parts of a mechanistic system.

Because cultures are complex, it is necessary to work on them systematically, but note the difference between a systems approach and a systematic cultural approach. In the latter you also have a model so that you can see where you are and where you are going in the change effort, and you have a checklist of influence areas and levels of implementation in order to assure that all important areas are covered. But, in contrast to the systems approach, people participate at each step. They are listened to, and their ideas are incorporated into the fabric of the change process where possible.

Some change specialists fear that involving many people of a wide range of talents, abilities, and experience in the change process will lower the level of thinking and water down the quality of the program. This possibility can be circumvented, however, if people are given an adequate opportunity, from the very beginning, to understand the nature of "culture" and the cultural change process and to identify the cultural norms affecting them. A variety of cultural change programs have proved that when people are given "ownership" of a program, they are far more capable of understanding and dealing with change than is ordinarily realized. It is crucial, therefore, to take the time needed at the outset of a change effort to help people see clearly the relationship between organizational cultures and cultural change influences.

WHAT IS CULTURE?

Culture can be an elusive concept because, on the one hand, we are all aware of its tyrannical power over us, but, on the other hand, we are often oblivious to its effect on our own behavior and perceptions.

As we examine the concept more closely, we see that sometimes the term *culture* is used in a broad way, referring to the American culture, Western culture, and so on. Sometimes it is used to refer to the arts and education, as in "He is a cultured gentleman." There are many definitions, and whole books have been written on the subject. In our work we define *culture* as "a more or less enduring constellation of forces within the group or organization that causes its members to respond in specific ways to a defined entity."[1] This definition encompasses the idea that cultures have a sustaining quality but are not permanently fixed.

Generally speaking, the term *culture* refers to any group of people who get together over a period of time with shared goals and values. A culture might be a corporation or a unit within a corporation. It might be as large as a whole community or as small as one family. It might be a whole school or a single classroom. In this book we are primarily concerned with the particular kind of culture we call *organizations*—broadly encompassing businesses, schools, communities, and large institutions. The lessons learned in dealing with organizational cultures like these, however, can carry over into other cultures—of family, neighborhood, social circles, and so forth.

In the same vein we talk about a "work environment" or a "social environment," and it is helpful sometimes to think in terms of macro- and microenvironments. These terms are relative: We can think of the American culture as a macroenvironment and the culture of one community or one corporation as a microenvironment within it. Or we can think of the corporation as a macroenvironment containing microenvironments of various departments and work teams.

The process of cultural change in any group, large or small, begins with a profound awareness of the immense impact of cultural norms.

NORMS, OUR BUILDING BLOCKS

The building blocks of our cultures are the norms that develop—those expected, accepted, and supported ways of behaving that determine so much of what we do.

Norms are a universal phenomenon. They are necessary, tenacious, but also extremely malleable. Because they can change so quickly and easily, they present a tremendous opportunity to people interested in change. Any group, no matter what its size, once it understands itself as a cultural entity, can plan its own

[1]Based on a definition of personality by Calvin S. Hall and Gardner Lindzey, in *Theories of Personality*, 2d ed. (New York: John Wiley, 1970).

norms, creating positive ones that will help it reach its goals and modifying or discarding the negative ones. And the group can do this despite what the outer culture is doing. You don't have to change the norms of the whole macroenvironment in order to change the norms of the microenvironment.

A person breaking a norm of a culture is usually penalized for it. Sometimes it is only through a raised eyebrow ("I wonder how he could have gotten a harebrained idea like that?"), or it may be a more severe reminder, such as being penalized for not having kept some fat in the budget for across-the-board percentage-type trimming—a practice that falls harder on the cooperative, conscientious person who has already trimmed than on the person who has taken this possibility into account and provided inflated figures. Norms and their accompanying sanctions are a determining factor in many situations of this type.

In large groups, such as communities, corporations, and school systems, each subculture or microenvironment has its own set of cultural norms (such as the "jocks" and "eggheads" of a typical high school). Some of these may overlap those of the larger social system, but they do not necessarily have to. The power of "culture" is found in the small cultural group as well as in the large.

ORGANIZATIONAL NORMS

Organizations, like all cultures, operate within a framework of norms that can either aid and abet their plans or be unseen obstacles to achievement. The task in a change project, briefly stated, is to help people understand the norms that are affecting their behavior, identifying at the outset of the program the particular norms that will be crucial to the changes sought. With this groundwork of normative analysis, implementation becomes a matter of confronting and dissipating negative norms and consciously installing positive norms in key influence areas. To maintain the norms that are needed for continued success, evaluation and renewal mechanisms are necessary. These are the basic steps of a culture-based change model, which is described more fully in chapter 2.

Since we live in a sea of norms, we need to be selective as we embark upon a change program, finding the norm areas that will be crucial to our success. It won't make too much difference to us if the norm is to wear a necktie, but it will make a tremendous difference if the norm is for individuals and departments not to cooperate with one another.

Generally we find that organizations have a crucial need for norms in the following areas:

Rewards and Recognition—What do we reward? What are the rewards? What things are given positive reinforcement? Do we punish people when they behave in the way we wish? Do we fail to give people permission to do the right thing?

Modeling Behavior—What kind of behavior are people modeling? Are our leaders modeling the behavior we ask for in our goals? What do people perceive as being modeled?

Confrontation—What kinds of things are confronted? How are they confronted? Are destructive win-lose tactics used? Is the norm to try to place the blame?

Communication and Information Systems—What is communicated? How is it communicated? Are there mixed messages? One-way communications? Is there adequate information flow about the important things?

Interactions and Relationships—Do people have adequate interaction with others who practice desirable norms? Do people treat each other with dignity and respect?

Training—What is trained for? How is the training conducted? Who does the training? How do people respond to the training? What skills do we need that we do not include in our training?

Orientation—Who is orienting new members of the group? How are they oriented? What kinds of norms do new members get introduced to?

Resources Commitment and Allocation—What is the level of commitment to change? What do we spend our money on? What are we willing to devote time to? What does assignment of personnel show about our real commitment?

Depending on the nature of the changes sought, other norm influence areas can be selected for examination. One company, for example, looked at the norms in these areas: organizational and personal pride, excellence of performance, teamwork and communication, leadership and supervision, profitability and cost effectiveness, associate relations, customer and consumer relations, honesty and security, training and development, innovation and change.

Whatever the key areas are, norms within it need to be identified clearly and discussed. Instruments have been developed (see chapter 4) to help people work with norms.

Using the cultural approach, people can begin to understand the underlying, unconscious patterns that are influencing their organizations. Although the emphasis on culture is new, the roots of this approach go back many years, stemming from the work of creative social scientists.

ROOTS OF THE CULTURAL APPROACH

Our particular approach to change is rooted in the work of many who came before us. Innovative thinkers such as Kurt Lewin, Abraham Maslow, and Erich Fromm have helped open our eyes to the power of the culture and to the tremendous possibilities for people-controlled change.

Lewin saw learning as a progressive discovery of structure either in the material to be learned or in the areas of experience. (For example: To learn to get someplace means to learn the structure of the route. To learn to achieve an organizational goal means to discover patterns of relationships involving members of the organization.) Lewin devised ways to analyze the life-spaces of individuals or groups and also contributed the concept of "barriers," or obstacles that obstruct behavior and keep us from doing what we want to do, whether we are aware of them or not.

Maslow's hierarchy of human needs pointed the way to an understanding of motivations within the corporate world. The satisfaction of these needs (progressively from security and comfort, through self-respect, to self-actualization) and his emphasis on peak experiences and their importance as models for what we can be, have proved invaluable.

Fromm's insights into the social nature of human beings provided groundwork for understanding the power of cultural forces and the necessity of coming to grips with them.

In the psychological field, a number of social learning theorists have contributed to our understanding of how individuals reciprocally react with their environments. Albert Bandura, for example, explained psychological functioning in terms of continuing reciprocal interaction of personal and environmental determinants. His social learning theory fostered an understanding of the importance of external factors in influencing individual behavior.

In the organization development movement, a number of practitioners have paid homage to the culture's power and pervasiveness and pointed out the necessity of dealing with it. Edgar Schein recognizes norms as "powerful controls of our behavior," and suggests that the process consultant "look at both the implicit and explicit norms of an organization, and see how they often contradict one another."[2] Warren Bennis, in listing eight principles for organization development, points out that "in undertaking any planned social change, the state of cultural readiness must be assessed," and sees this cultural readiness as "linked to the normative structure of the wider society," and an element that needs to be understood if the diagnosis is to be valid.[3] Douglas McGregor's descriptions of Theory X and Theory Y behaviors suggest the kinds of assumptions that underlie differing organizational patterns.[4] Robert Blake and Jane Mouton maintain that in order to help individuals, we must focus also on cultural considerations and recognize how deeply the culture of a corporation controls the behavior of all of its members.[5] Their gridwork has been helpful to us in making the possibilities of win-win solutions come alive to people.

Throughout the OD field, then, valuable insights have been expressed and techniques developed that have helped people to see how success with organizational change is linked to understanding cultural factors involved, as well as to appreciate the

[2]Edgar Schein, *Process Consultation: Its Role in Organization Development* (Reading, Mass.: Addison-Wesley, 1969).

[3]Warren Bennis, *Organization Development: Its Nature, Origins, and Prospects* (Reading, Mass.: Addison-Wesley, 1969).

[4]Douglas McGregor, *The Human Side of Enterprise* (New York: McGraw-Hill, 1960).

[5]Robert R. Blake and Jane Srygley Mouton, *The Managerial Grid* (Houston: Gult Publishing Company, 1964).

human aspects of the organizational situation. There has been a healthy exchange of ideas and techniques and a debate on the best possible ways to use them successfully. We have been fortunate to share in this activity as we developed our particular approach to change, which we call Normative Systems.

Many similarities exist between our approach and other OD efforts. The key difference lies in the emphasis we place on cultural considerations and on the practical, easily communicated methods that we have developed to deal with them. The assumption that organizations are cultures has led us to the following beliefs:

- It is not enough for managers and other leaders to understand the influence of culture; it is also essential that all the people in the organization share this understanding
- Culture is not a peripheral concern to be taken into account with a number of variables, but rather a central concern that underlies all of the other variables that influence the success of the change effort. (Thus interpersonal and sociotechnical change strategies are themselves culturally determined and therefore cannot exist as separate variables.)
- Group norms and norm influence areas are important components to work with.
- Systematic, planned change requires a multivariable, cultural approach throughout, in which all crucial areas are accounted for, with special attention to their oft-neglected cultural base.
- Cultural objectives, cultural achievements, cultural results, and cultural evaluations must undergird the OD effort if achievements are to be sustained.
- Participation in decision making by all the people affected is critical to planned cultural change, heightens motivation, and yields more lasting results.
- A basic framework for responsiveness to changing cultural problems and needs can help an organization move its style from one of rigidity to one of flexibility.

Our primary thesis is that if organizations think of themselves as cultures and focus on changing their cultural norms, the negative forces of the organizational unconscious can be dissipated, and meaningful change can be achieved and sustained.

One reason it has been so difficult to encourage a realistic focus on the depth and breadth of the culture's power is because Western society puts a strong emphasis on what we have come to call individuality. This focus on individual separateness has tended to result in higher levels of conformity. Because we have neglected to deal effectively with the power of group influences, they work on people without their being aware of what is happening to them. Thus people often feel they are "choosing" behavior when in fact they are merely conforming to the norms of the culture—outworn traditions that they have had little part in shaping.

As a result of this lack of awareness, people feel helpless in the grip of something outside themselves, without knowing what it is and without realizing that they can actually exercise a great deal of control over it.

As awareness of the culture is developed and people are provided with tools for shaping their environments, new and more profound levels of freedom and true individuality can be achieved.

CHIEF CONTRIBUTIONS

In the chapters ahead we offer what we feel are our most useful contributions to managers and others who are looking for answers to the questions raised earlier in this chapter. These contributions are, briefly, the following:

- a theory to help us become aware of the underlying obstacles that we meet when we try to make our organizations into what we want them to be
- a model that is useful in understanding and implementing the change process
- a four-pronged approach to installing change in day-to-day activities
- a method of dealing with objectives, measurements, and results on three levels, so that performance, programmatic, and cultural factors are all addressed
- a set of principles to guide any individual or group change program
- some recommendations regarding participatory democracy in our organizations, institutions, and communities
- some measuring instruments that make it possible to work practically and systematically with cultural norms
- a rational and practical guide for building supportive environments—for making our organizations more "open" and less "unconscious"

- a way to make small primary groups useful contributors to planned change
- an examination of the role of the organizational leader as a culture change agent

Primarily, what we have to offer is an approach to change that has been extremely helpful to us and to the people with whom we have worked. Our approach can be used in a number of different ways: as a comprehensive OD program or as a method of solving chronic problems, improving performance and productivity, resolving conflict, installing new programs, making old programs work, developing new organizations, or refurbishing old ones. In our work we make use of many techniques that we have drawn from the work of others, reordering them into a new and hopefully helpful framework. The cultural umbrella rides over everything, pulling other factors together under its shade. This happens not because the cultural view is the only view but because it has proved to be the most effective one in our experiences with people who are trying to make their organizations more successful.

chapter two
A Prescription
for Change

To change the organizational unconscious, we need to get beyond understanding and into action. Once the underlying currents are recognized, a way must be found to install changes and sustain them. In our prescription for change, we offer some practical guides:

- a four-phased model that encompasses the total change process
- three levels of goals—performance, programmatic, and cultural
- four dimensions to use in putting changes into practice in terms of the individual, the group, the leadership, and the overall policies of the organization

Each of these is discussed in more detail in the pages that follow.

A USEFUL FRAMEWORK

The model we have developed to deal with the organizational unconscious is the Normative Systems model for cultural change. It consists of four phases: discovery, involving people, bringing about change, and evaluating and renewing. This model is not kept in a back drawer or used only by leaders; it is shared with everyone affected by the change program. People need to know where they are and where they are going in the program, and their feeling of ownership depends a good deal on this.

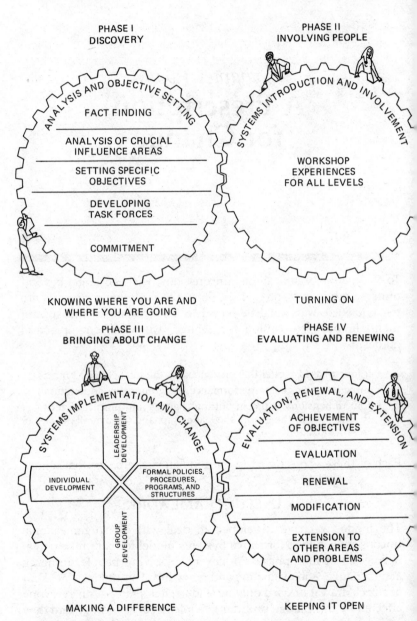

Figure 1. The Normative Systems Cultural Change Model. (Copyright 1976 by HRI Human Resources Institute.)

16

The conceptual framework we propose is a result of an interplay of many ideas and techniques. The Normative Systems model for cultural change grew out of our earlier experiences in urban areas. In the 1950s we had the opportunity to work with delinquent and predelinquent youngsters in Newark and New York City. During this experience we came to see the immense influence of the culture and developed some practical ways to help youngsters understand and make use of cultural influences to enhance their lives.

This led to work with Job Corps Centers, Peace Corps returnees, and various poverty program interventions. At approximately the same time, we began to work with a small supermarket company that had plans for extensive growth. The president of the company was fearful of losing the spirit, cooperation, and teamwork that had accounted for the success of the company in its early years. Would it be possible to maintain this same sense of excitement as the company moved from a three-store "chain" to one of the leading Fortune 500 companies?

Encouraged by our success in this effort, we moved to a number of other cultural settings: a large-scale program with migrant workers, an adult literacy effort, community improvement projects, schools, prisons, and hospitals. In all of them we found that basically the same thing was happening—people were trapped in their cultural patterns and did not know how to free themselves. Gradually there evolved the Normative Systems process, with which people were able to extricate themselves and make the kind of systematic changes they wanted in their lives.

The Normative Systems Model: A Brief Overview

Phase I.
Discovery
This first phase focuses on discovering and understanding the organizational unconscious and its influences. There is an analysis of the organizational culture, including identification of current cultural norms and a preliminary setting of objectives based on what the organization's members want it to be. This phase is one of fact finding and study, to assure that the change process is based on sound information. Norm instruments aid in identifying

existing norms and establishing the gap between what is and what is desired. In this way the unconscious patterns are brought into awareness. Levels of organizational support for certain behaviors are assessed. Key norm influences affecting the culture are discussed, choices are made, and goals are set. Objectives are set on the three levels mentioned above: performance, programmatic, and cultural. Once an analysis has been made and objectives set, the program can be tailored to the special needs and characteristics of the organization.

Phase II.
Involving People

Here the cultural change system is introduced to those directly affected, involving them in the change process. During this phase there is a special emphasis on cultural norms and cultural objectives. Participants get a clear idea of what norms are and what their normative objectives might be. They have an opportunity, usually in a high involvement workshop, to try out the kind of culture they desire and to begin to create an environment in which change can take place.

The workshop is organized into three parts: understanding, identifying, and changing. People learn about culture and the process by which cultural change takes place, they look at each change area and think about what they would like it to be, they learn to identify the norms that are affecting them in relation to the problems at hand, they begin to map out plans for individual and organizational change, and they have some direct experience with change as it affects their group's functioning. Usually an important element in that experience is in the realm of human relationships and openness, because one of the areas in which most organizations need help is how people relate to one another.

Phase III.
Bringing About Change

This is an implementation phase, during which the various elements of the organizational culture are systematically modified so that they can more effectively contribute to the achievement of objectives. During this stage four key elements are emphasized: individual development, work team or peer group development, leadership development, and the development of the policies, programs, and procedures of the culture. Specific change programs are usually required in each of these four elements, with each program being directed toward modifying the norm influences that have previously been identified. All three levels of goals are emphasized, with the cultural level particularly stressed so that not only are problems solved, but new ways of handling problems are built into the culture. Norm changes are put into practice within the day-to-day activities of the group and are reinforced by rewards and support systems.

Phase IV.
Evaluating and Renewing
The fourth phase provides ongoing feedback about the effectiveness of the change program. It includes reevaluation and renewal meetings, which continue as long as the change program is in effect. These meetings provide a periodic opportunity for members of the organization to review the positive norms, either to strengthen them or to modify them according to the changing times, and to lend further support to the internalization of skills dealing with both human and technical problems. Results on all three goal levels are evaluated. Extension to other areas of the organization or to other concerns is now possible and serves to strengthen achievement of the original project goals.

These four phases make up the basic process of any Normative Systems program. Whether the objective is to increase productivity on an assembly line, to achieve a more harmonious work force in an office, or to humanize a small committee or a whole community, the basic model is the same. Each step is important and cannot be omitted if change is to be successful and continuing.

We have found it very helpful in a change program for people to become familiar with this model early in the process, to have it available to them at all stages of the program. To see the process clearly conceptualized gives them greater confidence in their ability to change, and it is a motivational aid throughout the program to be able to see where one is and where one is going.

To install a systematic, cultural change program is to begin a process that is ongoing, self-evaluative, and self-renewing. It is not a simple panacea, and it involves much hard work, but our experience has been that when all parts of the system are accounted for and dealt with, meaningful change actually will come about, often at an amazing rate, and that it will be sustained.

Planning and Measuring Change: A Three-Level Process

Because the underlying cultural influences are so crucial in the achievement and maintenance of change, we have found it useful to plan and measure every change on three levels:

>Level I   Performance Results
>Level II   Programmatic Results
>Level III   Cultural Results

Level I encompasses the hard facts that must be carefully measured on an ongoing basis, the so-called bottom-line results, such as increases in profitability and production, reduction in quality problems or accidents, lower absenteeism figures, and increases in sales.

Most organizational leaders are familiar with Level I objectives because of the current concern for measurable achievement and the increased focus on performance data. Accompanying this concern, there has been an upsurge of knowledge and techniques for the measurement of organizational accountability. More and more companies have learned that specific objectives are necessary, and they take pains to provide measurements for them, seeking—and later, communicating—the results. This has been extremely helpful in situations where it has been well executed and has given people in organizations some measurable goals toward which they can be working.

The same is true also of the Level II objectives, which focus on the systematic tracking of programs. Programmatic actions, such as training programs, management-by-objectives seminars, zero-base budgeting procedures, and subsystems for compensation, evaluation, or communication, need to be tracked in terms of whether they do in fact come into being. Often measures are made in terms of the numbers participating, the action steps taken, or the numbers of programs in place.

Helpful as Level I and Level II objectives have often been, they have proved to have little lasting value without Level III objectives. Like a three-legged stool with only two legs functioning, we are thrown off balance. When we rely on performance objectives only, there can be some admirable bottom-line results, but there is a limited involvement of people in change, and the changes accomplished are not sustained. When we rely on programmatic objectives only, there may be a flurry of activity, with many people involved as the systems and programs are installed, but very little change takes place, and what does soon dissipates. When just these two—performance and programmatic objectives—are used, there may be impressive results for a while, but there is little likelihood that they will last.

While it is true, of course, that cultural changes will not take place or maintain themselves if the other two results areas are neglected, people are less familiar with the third type, and it therefore must usually be given greater emphasis. Unless the underlying cultures are modified, the bottom-line results and installation of programs and subsystems will have a short life.

To achieve the cultural norms we have as objectives, plans have to be set up just as they are for performance and programmatic objectives. These plans focus on developing positive cultural norms in areas intrinsic to the everyday life of the organization. Levels of organizational support can be measured by organizational support indicators similar to those described in the next chapter. If the key influence areas are not modified, the desired change probably will not "take," no matter how positive the initial results might seem. As we have pointed out, if people are to be penalized for practicing the "new behaviors," they will not be likely to continue them once they can find out a possible satisfactory alternative system to overcome them. But by working with norms and norm influence areas, people have been able to direct cultural change, and in fact most people are a great deal more capable of achieving these objectives than many organizational leaders assume.

A New Company Gets Results
The value of paying attention to the "third leg of the stool—cultural objectives—in a total organizational effort was demon-

strated recently when a new company that we were working with, a pharmaceutical manufacturer, used a systematic, culture-based approach from the start. The management team seleced to start the company was aware that high hopes and enthusiastic beginnings often give way to old, negative ways of doing things. They dealt with the three kinds of objectives, particularly seeing that positive cultural norms were installed from the beginning, with the following results:

Level I	Plant completed three months ahead of schedule, $8.4 million below budget
Level II	Effective systems installed and all employees taking part in their development: Corporate personnel Compensation Information Performance planning and review Orientation Training Criteria were met for each of these
Level III	The key norm influence areas selected for emphasis were reviewed, and norm indicators and organizational support indicators were administered to check on progress. There was particularly high achievement of positive norms in teamwork, communications, and pride in excellence. One area that had to be modified was compensation—it was found that rewarding individuals on an exclusive basis detracted from good teamwork norms, so extra rewards to teams were installed.

Results Are Not Only at the End

Results are not what happens at the end of a process, but are a vital ingredient almost from the very beginning. Furthermore, this early focus includes all three kinds of results. Later on, as a problem is worked on, an organization is developed, or a new program is installed, results on all three levels continue to be an important factor. They are evaluated in terms of the progress achieved and help provide motivation for further effort. Even when success is achieved, sustaining it is a matter of evaluating results on an ongoing basis and particularly of fortifying and strengthening cultural results to undergird the successes and make them permanent.

Although this takes hard work and a continuing concern, it is heartening to realize—and to see in action—that cultures are extremely malleable. This characteristic can be disastrous to change programs that don't recognize cultural forces, but can be a boon to programs that systematically and consciously deal with them. The culture's amazing resilience means that it can take on the new, planned, constructive norms within a short time and that helplessness and cynicism can be quickly replaced by realistic hope.

In summary, successful efforts develop good norms in these following areas:

- Involvement of all the people of the organization in helping set the three kinds of objectives and results measurements that have been described.
- Setting of realistic goals clearly stated and based on sound information. Checks are made to see that these goals are perceived clearly by the people affected.
- Focus on results that will benefit all parties concerned, not just one segment.
- And most importantly, emphasis on Level III cultural objectives, making certain that people follow through on changing key cultural norms.

The lessons learned in successful, systematic, culture-based efforts are applicable in a variety of different types of organizations, and the basic processes are essentially the same. In a supportive organizational environment the attention to results, at the beginning, the middle, and the never-ending end pays off in helping the organization, and its members achieve their goals.

Implementing Change
in Four Dimensions

For a successful organizational development program, every crucial influence area (as determined during the analysis phase) will need to be dealt with effectively on the four dimensions just mentioned: individual, group, leadership, and total organization. For example, let us suppose that recognition and rewards are seen as one of the most important items. Through a focus on the individual, positive steps are taken, with each person involved in seeing how his or her behavior could contribute to the norms in this area. Through a simultaneous focus on group development, support is given for the positive norms of this influence area. The group looks at things they are doing in rewarding and recognizing positive behavior. Through a focus also on leadership responsibility, leaders are helped to lend their support and to build the skills they will need to make this an everyday part of their leadership behavior. Finally, a focus on the total organization entails making changes in any policies, programs, and procedures that are adversely affecting positive rewards and recognition throughout the organization, making these regulatory influences supportive of positive norms.

Working with Individuals

Often in business organizations, the chief vehicle for implementing individual change is the performance planning and review system. Unfortunately, this procedure is often only a paper maneuver, or it consists of telling employees only what is wrong. But it can be a lot more. Effective organizations allow time for performance planning and review, and treat it as an important help in promoting change in day-to-day behavior. It is not a once-a-year formality, but an ongoing, everyday process.

In schools that wish to emphasize creativity, the review system might take the form of a teacher sitting down with a student and helping him or her establish goals for a personal program of change. This is quite different from the usual, "How are you doing in terms of repeating back the things I've asked you to repeat back?" (an unspoken negative norm).

Some schools are ensuring focus on the individual through use of the individual student contract. The student sets his or her own goals and makes a contract with the teacher or with fellow students. He or she is given a chance to modify and review these objectives as the semester proceeds. The reward may be in the form of grades or evaluations, or it may be in the form of recognition from teachers and classmates.

In a mental hospital, the performance-planning question might be, "How are you doing in meeting the goals you set for becoming more independent?" This is a reversal of the usual negative norm, "How are you doing in following the ward attendant's instructions?" If the hospital is truly a rehabilitation center, the individual's development toward autonomy is treated as an important goal to implement.

Another vehicle for individual change is the self-help module. In the Lifegain Positive Health Practices Program, for example, there are individual self-help modules available for exercise, weight and nutrition, stress reduction, safety, use of medical resources, alcohol and drug usage, and the development of better interrelationships. Each module contains content pieces that give background in the particular health area and that discuss the cultural influences that affect it, as well as exercises and planning sheets to help the individuals set their own goals, get their programs underway, and later evaluate their progress.

Focus on the Group

Our cultures are full of groups, often unorganized ones such as cliques and informal peer groups with no official status. The question is not whether or not we are going to have groups, but rather whether they are going to be recognized and listened to as part of the total change process. Employees in every organization have group meetings constantly—if not formal planned meetings, then informal ones over coffee breaks or in car pools.

Sometimes managers are fearful of groups forming. One president of a manufacturing company was horrified when we suggested that a system be set up for employees to get together on a formal basis. "I'm lucky my workers don't form groups," he said. "If they ever got together, I would never hear the end of it. There'd be nothing but gripes and complaints!" We pointed out the bar across the street from the main entrance to the plant. It was 4:00 P.M., and a shift had just let out. "There's where your meetings are already taking place," we said. "But that kind of meeting has no supervisor present and no way to deal with the negatives or deal with the issues that come up over and over again. How about setting up meetings that the company can get involved in?"

Since the groups are going to form anyway, it seems only logical—and more productive—to enlist their aid in the change process. Subcultures can make significant contributions to the larger culture and can help replace negative norms with the positive ones that have been agreed on. Formal, organized work teams can focus their energy on accomplishing the agreed-upon goals and can be a powerful help in establishing new norms. In fact, helping the work team develop a positive culture is probably the most important way for sustaining change in the business or industrial organization. Since every worker is part of a work team of some sort—from the board of directors to the smallest department in the business—attention to the group level is a crucial factor in the change process.

Leadership Development

In the implementation phase of a cultural change process, leadership development is a key area of emphasis. Without effective leadership, no change program is likely to succeed. Unfortunately, little attention is given in most organizations to the development of leadership skills and understandings.

To overcome this deficiency, leadership development modules are available. They help leaders examine their roles and the norms that pertain to them, as well as help them systematically to make the changes they feel are important. Modules in this series (see appendix A) cover such subjects as elements of leadership, assumption of responsibility, support and confrontation, performance appraisal, involvement and motivation, communication and information systems, and how to be an effective trainer. Normative instruments, charts, and forms for understanding and implementing the leadership development system are included.

In addition, the norm indicator on leadership (appendix C) is a valuable tool to use during implementation as well as in analysis and evaluation. It can be a guide to the type of changes that need to be put into effect on the job, as well as a way of checking on progress in making those changes.

The role of the leader as a cultural change agent will be covered more thoroughly in chapter 7.

Looking at the Total Organization

Implementing change on the organizational level means examining the policies, programs, and procedures of the organization and seeing what changes can be made to remove obstacles to goals and to facilitate the growth of the new desired norms. Many times organizational structures support prior forms of behavior that are no longer valid for either employee or management in light of the changes sought.

Sometimes the problem is not so much a matter of bringing about changes as clarifying what *is*. Such things as sick-leave guidelines or time-in/time-out systems sometimes need to be better understood and made effective throughout the organization. If these policies are well communicated and if feedback on them is encouraged so that people have a chance to air all grievances and ask questions, then the policies will be more effective.

Specific programs to examine the written directives of the culture sometimes have to be undertaken in order to ensure their positive relationship to organizational goals. Task forces can be formed to implement the necessary changes and suggest ways of overcoming obstacles that might arise. In a real estate office, for example, agents from one region were competing heavily against agents from another region in order to get a bigger proportion of the allotted company bonuses. A task force recommended that the reward system be changed so that a salesperson who sent a client to another region would share in the rewards.

In a school, the homework system, the course scheduling procedures, and the disciplinary rules might all need to be reviewed. In a business, the budgets, manuals, policy statements, programs, and promotion procedures are among the items the task force would need to look over very carefully in order to recommend changes.

While at first glance this might seem an area in which top managers would assume responsibility, actually it is more effective to have a task force that cuts across all levels of the hierarchy, for all people will bear the brunt of poor procedures, and all will benefit if more effective ones are installed.

chapter three
Guidelines
That Humanize

In successful cultural change programs, certain key principles undergird the total change process, helping the organizational unconscious to become an integrating, humanizing force. By adhering to these principles on all levels and in all situations, people can erase the destructive patterns that have impeded meaningful change.

Although the principles may vary in emphasis from program to program, there are eight important ones that are usually involved. When effectively implemented, these become a way of life within the organization and serve as ongoing criteria that can be used to determine the appropriateness of various actions being considered.

General Principles of Cultural Change
- involving people in the problems and programs affecting them
- using win-win, non-blame-placing approaches
- having clarity of goals, objectives, purposes, and tasks
- focusing on results, both short- and long-range
- working from a sound information base
- being systematic and using multilevel change strategies
- integrating concern for people and achievement
- emphasizing sustained culture change

When these principles become norms of the change process, the result is a democratic, participatory, flexible change program that can bring about and maintain the cultural changes being sought.

PRINCIPLES AS NORMS

Guiding principles are often statements that appear in public reports and planning documents only to be disregarded when the action program begins. To avoid this, it is important that they receive the same cultural attention as the programmatic goals that are established and that they do in fact become the norms or everyday way of doing things throughout the total change program.

This is particularly important because of the fact that such principles are frequently not the norm when the change program is first introduced. If they are to become the norm, specific steps will need to be taken from the outset. If, for example, win-win solutions are to be the watchword of the change program, the program leaders and consultants need to model that behavior in their own day-to-day interactions. If sound information is to be required as a program principle, the program leadership cannot violate this principle in its rush to cut corners in getting things done.

In order that the guiding principles become the norms of the change project, it is important that supportive environments be created for them—that is, that people be praised and rewarded for their use rather than penalized or criticized. Similarly with confrontation. It is important that negative norms be confronted creatively, so that blame placing is avoided but the negative norm is dealt with nonetheless. Rather than an accusation that "John was making promises he isn't ready to deliver," a look at the norms of the group is in order: "Is this a place where it is expected and accepted to make promises rather than working for results? If so, what can we do to change that norm?"

Some of the norms that most often get in the way of effective implementation of such principles are norms of:

- looking for simplistic, one-level solutions
- blaming others, finding fault, and particularly blaming the victim
- proceeding on the basis of inadequate information, wishful thinking, or well-intentioned myths
- leaving it up to the other fellow, especially the experts
- trying to do it all by one's self without involving others
- making promises and not delivering results
- helplessness, believing that people can't really change, that "it's just human nature" and "you can't fight City Hall"
- false individualism, seeing difficulties and solutions only in individual terms

Applying the positive principles of the program can help dissipate these negative norms. Let us look more closely at the principles, with special attention to the first one, which deals with the involvement of people.

INVOLVING PEOPLE IN CHANGE

Are People Resistant to Change?

We hear a lot about people being resistant to change, but this resistance is usually resistance to changes that are being foisted upon them without their participation in its development. Most of us are eager to participate in change that we ourselves create, particularly when that creative activity is shared with others.

A large, prestigious manufacturing company gave its employees generous benefits—expensive, paid vacations; expanded insurance benefits; a generous pension plan. The buildings were beautiful, the equipment was the latest. No one was ever fired or laid off. Yet a routine morale survey showed that employee morale was at a low ebb. The same corporation started a new division in another location. People on all levels from top management to the lowest hourly employee were, from the moment they joined the company, encouraged to help plan the kind of organization they would like to have. Their ideas and suggestions were listened to, and many were carried out. The term *associate* was used, rather than *employee*, to serve as a reinforcement of the idea that "ownership" belonged to everyone who worked there. Morale was high and was sustained, and the plant opened ahead of schedule on a lower budget than had been anticipated.

What was the difference? It was due in large part to the involvement of people in the decisions that would affect their lives.

Of the many variables that must be considered in organizational development, the "people variable" is well worth highlighting. Unless people who would be affected by the proposed change are involved in it, that change may be strenuously resisted, and if accomplished, may not be sustained.

The Importance of Involvement and Participation

The involvement of people in planning and executing the changes that will affect them is often the necessary ingredient to getting past obstacles to change. Let's see how participation affects some of the most common obstacles.

LACK OF MOTIVATION.
Positive motivation stems, to a great extent, from people "owning" a project. If it is ours, we want to help to make it work.

HELPLESSNESS.
When we feel powerless because authorities above us or pressures outside us seem to be in charge, telling us what to do and how to do it, we think things can't change. When we are listened to and our ideas are acted upon, we no longer feel this stultifying helplessness.

LACK OF TIME AND MONEY.
Often the necessary time and money are lacking for successful change programs because the involvement of certain key groups has been neglected. If people do not feel themselves to be a part of the change process, they are unlikely to be willing to invest their time and money in it or the time and money that they have decision-making power over (as in the case of taxpayers or boards of directors).

CONFORMITY.

The authoritarian type of leader who imposes ideas on those below him or her while espousing participation or democratic ideals is an anachronism in most change programs. But we are often left with more subtle manipulations, in which people are not treated as individuals but are forced into molds. Listening to them, getting feedback on what is happening—involving people in the flow of information about what is really going on—is an antidote to conformity.

LACK OF ENERGY AND
CREATIVE ENTHUSIASM.

The excitement and energy that keep a program going cannot be maintained if people don't feel involved in what is happening. But enthusiasm is renewed when people are involved, when the door is always open to the new idea and there is continuing commitment to hearing and carrying out the suggestions that they agree are worthwhile.

What Kind of Participation?

In our work we have found it essential for a successful change program to have people involved from the very beginning and throughout the total process. They are part of the analysis, the setting of goals, the making of plans, the executing of those plans, and the evaluation, renewal, and extension activities. Leaving them out in any of these phases can doom a program to failure. A large organization might involve people in analyzing its needs, for example, and may even have exciting goal-setting sessions where plans are made for change. But then the report is filed, people return to their desks, and things go on much the same way. The implementation of the plans is put back into the hands of a few— "Let George do it"—and the sense of excitement is lost. Participation, to be a valuable force, must be continual.

Participation also means that people "own" the program. This feeling of ownership is an important motivating force. The most successful organizations are those that are "owned" by all of the people and not just the people at the top. This ownership must be a fact as well as a feeling. Leaders must see the change process as being owned by all who participate in it and must not merely give lip service to ownership as a manipulatory device. Conversely, it sometimes happens that a leader believes in widespread owner-ship but the people don't feel it. "It's *your* program," he or she might say, frustrated when the health program the company has bought is limping along with little participation. The people don't feel they own the program, in this case, because they have not really been involved in its development—it was handed to them like a welfare check.

Many employees of organizations are embarrassed to use the term *my company*, thinking that the leaders of the company will think they are being too pushy. What is lacking is a verbal, public commitment to the idea of ownership from the leadership—carried out in action in its policies and procedures.

Carrying out this commitment must be done sincerely, with-out faking it. There are probably some decisions the managers are already set in and have no choice about; for example, in most profit-making corporations the managers are not going to have a choice about whether or not they will try to make profits, so there is no point in pretending that people have that decision to make. However, there are open choices about how the organization will go about its work. It is important for managers to be clear with people about what the real choices are; if there is pretense, the whole effort will be undercut.

Involvement means intelligent involvement, based upon peo-ple understanding what the change program is all about and being aware of the cultural norms that are going to help it succeed or drag it to defeat. If people are to be part of the decision-making process, they need to be given the skills and training to make intelligent decisions based on sound information. Participation should not be blind, but knowledgeable.

For example, people often want to be involved in setting their objectives, yet feel they lack the knowledge and skills to do so. In this case, it is necessary to develop those skills until they feel comfortable with the process. This can be true of people at any level of the organization—even presidents of corporations and heads of government bodies may lack those skills.

The amount of authority, power, and responsibility that will go with participation will depend upon the situation and basic structure of the organization. In hierarchical organizations there is never a total equality in these areas. But there can be equality in the areas of listening, feedback, and information flow. There can be two-way communication, where people on lower levels of the hierarchy feel supported in offering their ideas to those above them, and people on the higher levels do not hand down pronouncements without first finding out what those below them think and feel about the proposed change.

The excitement of people who have just created something together was illustrated recently in a supermarket OD. program. Here a group had just created a new display together and were pleased with their effort and its effect on the customers. This same kind of excitement can be seen when teachers create a new curriculum together or tailor an exciting curriculum to their needs. Contrast this with the feeling of being told that a new curriculum created by someone else is to be implemented by them whether they like it or not.

When people are involved in the process, they have a greater commitment to the outcome. When we tap into our creativity, using building rather than blocking techniques, we open people up to something meaningful and exciting—a fertile ground for lasting cultural change to take root.

Pitfalls of the Participation Idea

The idea of people involvement as a management technique is not without its problems. In the organizational development literature we find warnings about participative decision making. Chris Argyris talks about the "misplaced emphasis" in the recent push toward participation by employees in organizations, by citizens in communities, and by students in schools. "The idea," he explains, "was to give these groups more power in the decision-making process. This policy overlooked the fact that such participation would probably increase the number of people with Model I assumptions [learning systems that inhibit the detection and correction of error], who, in turn would create even more complicated learning systems."[1] This very real problem can, in our

[1]Chris Argyris, "Double Loop Learning in Organizations," *Harvard Business Review*, 55, no. 5 (September-October 1977), pp. 122-23. Reprinted with permission of the *Harvard Business Review*. Copyright 1977 by the President and Fellows of Harvard College, all rights reserved.

experience, be averted by simultaneous attention to other variables: sound information, proper skills, and results orientation. The problem is not whether or not to have participation, but the quality and form of the participation. People need to understand the culture and identify the cultural norms affecting the problem before they are called upon to develop action programs for change.

The pitfalls of the people involvement concept do not destroy its validity. Rather, these pitfalls suggest just how important it is that other variables be considered and dealt with simultaneously and in coordination with one another.

In the paragraphs that follow, we will briefly discuss some of the other key principles and some norms relating to their implementation.

NO-FAULT APPROACHES

Rather than trying to find out who's to blame for problems, the emphasis needs to be on finding solutions by which everyone will benefit. In a well-conceived norm change program, problem solving without blame placing is a constructive asset.

When all parties are encouraged to deal with problem behavior as it is related to norms, there is minimal risk of arousing personal defenses. It is easier to take the criticism, "The norm around here is to arrive fifteen minutes late to a meeting; can we change it?" than it is to take, "You guys are always holding up the meeting."

Tied to this approach to problem solving is a second one: avoiding a focus on what *others* can do, instead of what *we* can do together, to bring about change. Most problems require that each individual examine his or her own behavior in relationship to the group's objectives. People are more likely to do this when the focus is on achieving results and modifying the culture rather than on finding out who is to blame for what has occurred. This tends to free energy formerly wasted in win-lose confrontations and to spark enthusiastic movement toward change. Therefore, it is productive to shift away from creating environments where people cannot succeed and then blaming them for failure and to move toward creating success environments that will help people become winners.

Power and Values:
Through a Normative Lens

Related to blame-placing conflicts are the issues of power and values. In a systematic, cultural approach we look at these often-elusive issues with our "normative eyeglasses" on. We ask ourselves, What are the norms concerning power in the organization? Do people expect to have power struggles between management and labor? Is it the norm for people in lower positions to feel powerless?

Norms concerning helplessness are expressed frequently in standard jokes such as:

> "The more things change, the more they remain the same."
> "We've had our war on poverty—and we lost."
> "A new management? It's just the chiefs upstairs changing blankets again."
> "You can't fight City Hall—you just have to live with it."

Again and again in organization development programs, such norms of powerlessness have proved to be severe obstacles to getting the program off the ground.

Though we speak jokingly of our inability to change, it is no joke when it continues to happen to us over and over again. The frustration of seeing what we think are "results" shine out like Fourth of July fireworks and then as quickly die off leads to a chronic cynicism among many groups. The destructive buildup of feelings of helplessness frequently proves even more harmful to the achievement of long-range objectives than if there had been no "results" at all.

However, once these attitudes are seen as cultural norms rather than as permanent states of being (as group expectations rather than individual habits of mind), then they can be overcome.

In a similar fashion the values we want become more attainable when seen as norms created by the group. Although there is a difference of opinion about what a value is, basically the term is used to speak of an abstract thing held to be of worth by an individual over a period of time. In this definition we can see that the values of a group or organization are very much dependent on the normative structure and influences within that organization.

When people try to modify their values without taking into account the norms of the culture, they are unlikely to be successful. In chapter 8 we describe a number of unsuccessful efforts in doing exactly that.

In all of this it is not our contention that power systems and values are unimportant but rather that they are intrinsically intertwined with the norms that make up cultural patterns of the organization.

CLARITY

Not only should goals, objectives, purposes, and tasks be clear, but they need to be stated in specific terms, with the group frequently checking back to make sure members have a clear understanding. Openness of communication becomes a watchword for assuring such clarity.

In successful cultures, the goals and purposes are kept constantly in view as the change process develops and work gets underway in installing and sustaining positive new norms. People in one department or one segment of the culture share their objectives with other departments or segments and have an opportunity to receive help and feedback. In the course of this process, objectives may be modified or people's perceptions of them sharpened.

Continued use of the cultural change model is helpful in keeping people clear about where they are in relation to the total program.

RESULTS, NOT MERE PROMISES

Rather than focusing on promises or on mere activities, the norm needs to be that people search for solutions and are oriented to achieving results. Without this focus on results, we get caught up in abstractions and unfulfilled promises. If we focus on results—on what we actually do—the excitement of achievement begins to feed on itself.

Continuing emphasis on results not only replaces empty promises, it also replaces the negative norm of blaming. Finger-pointing behavior is bypassed when the orientation is toward accomplishment and concrete results. The negative norm of helplessness is also undermined, for the realization that something is being accomplished spurs people on. Attention can be paid to excellence and to solving the next part of the problem, and there is a feeling of being in control. Many people at first don't really think that change is possible, but they can be convinced that things can happen when they actually see some results begin to appear.

Successful change programs set specific, measurable short- and long-range goals that everyone agrees will constitute satisfactory cultural change. The short-range goals need to be ones that can be achieved in a reasonable period of time and that lead to early, visible results.

The long-range goals must also be clearly defined, for mere "activities" that aren't framed in the larger context are, in the long run, as disappointing as meaningless promises. Both immediate and continuing actions must be planned since early success in modifying a culture motivates continued efforts.

Visibility of results is a crucial factor. In effective change programs, results are regularly and promptly reported in a manner that people throughout the organization can understand. Results that do not have naturally high visibility can be highlighted by good feedback and information systems.

Reports on results have the greatest impact when they are positioned in the larger framework of agreed-upon objectives and are seen as progress toward shared organizational goals. Data about accomplishments, if fed back regularly, will keep people in touch with progress toward objectives and give confidence and support to those who initially became committed to work toward change. They will also help convince the skeptical.

A SOUND INFORMATIONAL BASE

Rather than hunches, wishful thinking, or so-called common sense, we need to put the program on a sound data base, gathering together whatever information is necessary to do this. This information needs to be shared willingly throughout the organization. In many organizations, the negative norm of holding information to oneself or within the department is the greatest obstacle to organizational harmony.

Unfortunately, our cultural norms typically emphasize the development of solutions even before we have clearly identified the problems. Thus, in one change program that dealt with drug use among teenagers, the assumption was made that all teenagers were involved in direct drug use. However, a later study revealed that less than 5 percent of this particular group were directly involved, and so the nature of the program had to be changed.

A similar insight was gained from an analysis of child labor among migrant workers. This revealed that low worker income and lack of child care facilities were the problem rather than parental attitudes, as had previously been surmised. Greater parental productivity and adequate child care facilities made the "insurmountable" problem quite easy to solve.

As we saw in chapter 2, three kinds of information are needed for developing target goals: (1) "hard-line" data—factual, quantifiable data that can be used to measure progress; (2) programmatic information—that is, facts about the extent to which proposed actions are being carried out; and (3) cultural information covering what the norms are, how strong they are, what is actually happening in the organization, as contrasted with what is supposedly or officially happening.

SYSTEMATIC, MULTILEVEL APPROACHES

Even with cultural problems that seem relatively simple on the surface, it is necessary to approach them on several levels simultaneously rather than relying on simple, single-variable solutions. Openness and flexibility need to be the norm. A systematic approach, in which all the important variables are under scrutiny at once, can get us past the barrier of helplessness. Usually there are several key pressure points in a change situation at which effective work can bring about the desired change. The way to success is to attack problems intelligently and systematically, working on the important pressure points in a coordinated way.

In building positive norms in this area it is important to realize that we live in a society where people are taught from childhood to approach most problems in highly simplistic ways. The phase "All you need to do is . . ." is an almost stock problem-solving answer in many groups, organizations, and communities. It has been our experience that no matter what "solution" is suggested for the end of that sentence, it is likely to be insufficient. Cultural problems are usually the result of complex variables, and their solution will require systematic and creative attention to a number of such variables if successful and sustained changes are to take place.

INTEGRATING CONCERN FOR PEOPLE AND ACHIEVEMENT

Too often concern for people and concern for achievement are seen as opposing goals. If people are involved in decisions, satisfied with their jobs, and happy about the quality of their work environment, it is going to have a salutary effect on overall achievement. Conversely, gratifying results and recognition for their part in achieving them will enhance people's feelings about themselves and their work. Whenever these two goals appear to be in conflict, it is helpful to point out to people—perhaps through the use of the grid chart (page 68)—that ways need to be found to resolve the conflict and get on with mutually beneficial solutions.

SUSTAINED CULTURAL CHANGE

Instead of treating symptoms, the group needs to deal with root causes and try to develop norms of support that will be long lasting. If we really want to change, we must be willing to commit ourselves to an effort that will extend over a long period of time, for negative norms are often deep-rooted, and building support for positive ones is crucial. Often it would be better not to start a program at all than to start it when we are not prepared to continue with it.

In an organization or community, this recognition of a sustained effort is particularly important, for there are many levels to reach and many people to involve. The necessity for a long-term effort need not be discouraging, however, if coupled with simultaneous work on achieving immediate results in some areas.

INTERLOCKING PRINCIPLES AND NORMS

The norms of all these areas are interlocking, reinforcing each other. Look, for example, at how the other seven affect the first crucial principle of people involvement. Without win-win, non-blame-placing approaches, many people are going to get turned off. Without clarity of tasks and goals and plans, increased involvement may only muddy the waters and impede progress. Without a focus on results, greater people involvement could result in a complexity of undirected and unconnected activities. Without a sound information base, involving more people might merely involve them in more wasted effort. Without a systematic, multi-level approach, important aspects would be likely to be forgotten. Without integrating concerns for both people and achievement, an emphasis on one or the other can throw the program off balance. Without sustained commitment, follow-through, and deep cultural change, we would only have greater numbers of frustrated and disillusioned people.

Since the process itself is as important as the goal, the principles need to be built in from the very beginning. If they are followed throughout all phases of the systematic program, the chances of making the desired changes and sustaining them are very great indeed. Dealing in this way with the organizational unconscious provides us with a sound theoretical framework for organizational intervention. Moreover, the practical results are rewarding and lasting.

chapter four
Tools for Understanding Organizational Cultures

Seen from a cultural vantage point, the success of an organization depends upon its ability to understand the norms that are influencing it and the levels of organizational support that exist in particular norm areas. This understanding is essential throughout all four phases of the change process.

Instruments that deal with norms are therefore important both as data collection and as teaching tools. The two instruments we have found most useful are the *support barometer* and *"As I See It...,"* a norm indicator. Both of these measure perceptions—and it is perceptions that are the important issue. The support barometer is designed to measure the perceived level of organizational support that exists for specific norm goals. "As I See It..." helps us to get at the norms observed by organizational members. In addition, both instruments are useful as teaching tools to help people sharpen their cultural perceptions.

THE SUPPORT BAROMETER

The simpler of the two instruments is the support barometer. It is designed to secure people's perceptions of the levels of support that exist for particular actions or behaviors within the organization. It asks people to check off on a scale the level of support or nonsupport that they perceive for a particular behavior or action. The instrument can cover a wide range of organizational issues. It can be conducted entirely around a single issue, such as absenteeism, health, or a sense of community—whatever issue is seen to be paramount. It can be done as a small survey—as in board meetings or committee meetings—or can be done with a large department or the whole organization. It is relatively easy to administer and is easily scored.

SUPPORT BAROMETER
FOR HEALTH PRACTICES*

How well is our organization doing in actively, constructively, and consistently supporting people in their efforts to:

	VERY WELL	WELL	SOME, BUT NOT ENOUGH	POOR	VERY POOR
1. engage in a regular, planned program of physical exercise?	1	2	3	4	5
2. stop smoking?	1	2	3	4	5
3. understand the effect of stress and what can be done to avoid its negative impact on personal health?	1	2	3	4	5
4. achieve their correct weight and maintain it on a sustained basis?	1	2	3	4	5
5. understand and follow sound nutritional practices, including the eating of a nutritious breakfast every day?	1	2	3	4	5
6. avoid the overuse of caffeine, saccharine, sugar, salt, and cholesterol-producing foods?	1	2	3	4	5
7. avoid the overuse and misuse of alcohol?	1	2	3	4	5
8. avoid the overuse and misuse of drugs?	1	2	3	4	5

*Copyright 1978 by HRI Human Resources Institute.

	VERY WELL	WELL	SOME, BUT NOT ENOUGH	POOR	VERY POOR
9. have regular medical and dental examinations or health screenings and follow the recommendations given?	1	2	3	4	5
10. maintain their proper blood pressure?	1	2	3	4	5
11. employ sound health knowledge and maintain sound health practices?	1	2	3	4	5
12. follow sound safety practices at home, at work, and on the highway?	1	2	3	4	5
13. understand the importance of good mental health and deal effectively with mental health and emotional problems?	1	2	3	4	5
14. develop and maintain positive human relations in their day-to-day activities?	1	2	3	4	5
15. realize their fullest potential as human beings?	1	2	3	4	5

Here you can see an organizational support barometer related to health promotion. The following support barometers show how the instruments can be used in dealing with teamwork issues and total organizational development.

SUPPORT BAROMETER
FOR TEAMWORK*

To what extent are the following practices and behaviors supported in the organization:

*Copyright 1978 by HRI Human Resources Institute.

	COMPLETELY	TO A GREAT EXTENT	TO SOME EXTENT	TO A LIMITED EXTENT	NOT AT ALL
1. Emphasizing cooperation over competition	1	2	3	4	5
2. Getting people to see themselves as part of a common work effort	1	2	3	4	5
3. Coordinating each group's work with that of other groups in the organization	1	2	3	4	5
4. Encouraging people to be supportive of each other	1	2	3	4	5
5. Organizing and scheduling time and resources effectively	1	2	3	4	5
6. Being fair and equitable in the distribution of work that needs to be done	1	2	3	4	5
7. Seeing that work efforts are well coordinated	1	2	3	4	5
8. Seeing that teamwork is something that is actually carried out rather than something that is just talked about	1	2	3	4	5
9. Rewarding people for collaboration and teamwork	1	2	3	4	5
10. Stopping departmental parochialism	1	2	3	4	5
11. Bringing up problems or other unpleasant issues in constructive ways	1	2	3	4	5
12. Providing positive feedback	1	2	3	4	5
13. Ensuring that individuals and groups listen to each other, particularly when they are in disagreement	1	2	3	4	5
14. Encouraging people to see their team's work as part of a systematic, cultural effort	1	2	3	4	5

SUPPORT BAROMETER FOR TOTAL ORGANIZATION DEVELOPMENT*

To what extent are the following practices and behaviors supported in the organization:

*Copyright 1981 by HRI Human Resources Institute.

	COMPLETELY	TO A GREAT EXTENT	TO SOME EXTENT	TO A LIMITED EXTENT	NOT AT ALL
1. Regularly planning and reviewing work goals and the progress made toward their accomplishment	1	2	3	4	5
2. Scheduling in regular and constructive feedback on how people are doing	1	2	3	4	5
3. Seeing that each person has an opportunity to be a member of an effective team	1	2	3	4	5
4. Having work groups meet regularly to deal with important issues and develop ways to improve effectiveness	1	2	3	4	5
5. Seeing that organizational programs, policies, and procedures are clear, understood, helpful, up-to-date, and reviewed regularly	1	2	3	4	5
6. Seeing that people get the information they need to do their jobs	1	2	3	4	5
7. Actively seeking out the ideas and opinions of others	1	2	3	4	5
8. Making orientation a helpful preparation for the on-the-job experience	1	2	3	4	5
9. Assuring that training programs are effective in giving people the knowledge and skills they need to do their jobs well	1	2	3	4	5
10. Maximizing the effectiveness of the human resources available	1	2	3	4	5
11. Making selection and promotion practices fair and equitable	1	2	3	4	5
12. Providing a clear way of measuring results as an ongoing part of organizational life	1	2	3	4	5
13. Achieving a fair and even distribution of the work that needs to be done	1	2	3	4	5
14. Looking for solutions rather than for someone to blame	1	2	3	4	5
15. Building supportive cultural environments	1	2	3	4	5

	COMPLETELY	TO A GREAT EXTENT	TO SOME EXTENT	TO A LIMITED EXTENT	NOT AT ALL
16. Using creative approaches to problem solving	1	2	3	4	5
17. Using all problems as training opportunities	1	2	3	4	5
18. Assuring effective teamwork between individuals and departments	1	2	3	4	5
19. Involving people in the decisions affecting them	1	2	3	4	5
20. Focusing on the achievement of results rather than on the implementation of activities	1	2	3	4	5
21 Building win-win solutions for problem solving	1	2	3	4	5
22. Taking systematic approaches to the development of change programs	1	2	3	4	5

In its application to health-related norms, the first support barometer illustrated here asks respondents to identify how well their organizations are doing in "actively, constructively, and consistently providing support" for people in their efforts to change in fifteen different areas of health (exercise, smoking, etc.) and scores the organization on whether it is doing *very well*, *well*, *some but not enough*, *poorly*, or *very poorly* in providing support.

Because of the perceived lack of support for positive health practices in most organizations, the instrument usually brings forth low ratings in this area. The overall ratings for one company are shown in figure 2. You will note that "poor" and "very poor" ratings account for more than 80 percent of the responses.

The organizational support barometer is a way of analyzing needs for organizational support at the beginning of a program and keeping track of the levels of continued support that are perceived

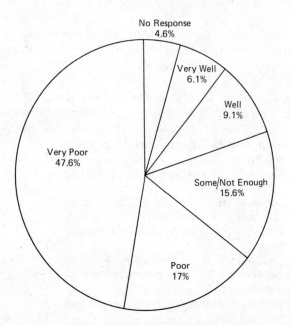

No Response
4.6%

Very Well
6.1%

Well
9.1%

Some/Not Enough
15.6%

Poor
17%

Very Poor
47.6%

Figure 2. "Is Your Company Helping You to Health?"
(Perceived Company Support for Good Health Practices
in a Large Corporation.)

by members of the organization over a period of time. When the
levels of support are low, it indicates that intensive action may be
necessary.

Significant shifts are possible as successful programs are
introduced. The barometer is very sensitive to change and makes a
good indicator of the program's success at any given time. When
the perceived levels of support begin to drop off, it can provide an
early warning system revealing that the newly adopted positive
norms may be weakening.

"AS I SEE IT..."

Another instrument that has been widely used in our cultural
change programs is "As I See It . . . ," a norm indicator. Since the
collection of norm data plays an important role in the success of an

organizational effort, the instrument that collects that data warrants careful consideration. It must be relatively easy to administer and simple enough for people at all levels of the organization to understand, particularly when a change effort involves people from many different backgrounds. Yet the instrument must be of sufficient complexity to account for a number of crucial variables, give enough data to be useful, and be specific enough to clear up ambiguities.

Because the cultural aspect of our lives has been generally neglected, it is still an area of uncertainty. As Jay Galbraith, an OD specialist, has pointed out: "The greater the uncertainty, the greater the amount of information that must be processed among decision-makers during task execution in order to achieve a satis-factory level of performance."[1] In working with cultural forces, detailed breakdowns of what appear on the surface to be widely accepted generalities are going to be necessary. Despite all of this, the instrument must be concise, so that data collection and interpretation do not become a burden and decision makers are not overloaded with more information than they can handle.

The instrument we call "As I See It..." (see appendix B for a complete copy of this norm indicator) has been designed to meet this criterion and has proved its usefulness in diverse settings for more than ten years.

The emphasis is again on perceptions, for it is people's perceptions of norms that change them. For example, in one department, 90 people out of 100 might be exaggerating their budget figures, and members of the department would see it as the norm; in another, only 10 out of 100 might be doing it, but again it might be seen as the norm. The important thing is not the actual behavior or the prevalence of certain behaviors, but people's perception of them.

Because "As I See It...," like most instruments of its type, is an imperfect tool, it needs to be accompanied by observations and interviews. It is most valuable when used with some common sense. Often the instrument is used as a teaching tool to help people sharpen their own perceptions and become aware of the power of norm influences in their lives. The most helpful norm

[1] Jay Galbraith, *Designing Complex Organizations* (Reading, Mass: Addison-Wesley, 1973), p.4.

indicators are the ones people make up themselves to fit the particular needs of their organization. The norm indicator provided in appendix B can serve as a model instrument for organizations that wish to create their own.

Basic Features

"As I See It..." is essentially a perceptual survey consisting of normative statements that have been selected as key indicators of the success, or lack of it, of an organizational culture. These statements reflect norms that may or may not exist in the culture being surveyed.

The language of the statements reflects an interest in behavior, for if we are going to change behavior, we need an instrument that contrasts what is perceived as happening with what might ideally happen. Furthermore, because cultural change focuses on group behavior, the instrument is carefully worded to ask what individuals see as occurring in their group or organization, rather than what they see themselves as doing.

Sometimes the norm influence areas are culled down to the eight most important ones, for many managers find this easier to handle. Actually, any combination of influence areas can be used, depending on the needs of the particular organization.

No matter whether the approach is to take the basic indicator and adapt it or to construct a new one from scratch, there is an advantage to reviewing the categories of the basic indicator at some point early in the process. This can help to surface some latent patterns that are causing problems.

Taken one at a time, the statements used in a norm indicator often seem unimportant and rather simple. After all, they are easily understood statements about behaviors we are likely to see around us all the time. So it often surprises people when they find out that these statements, added up, give them a guide to what they can do to make some hitherto elusive changes in their social environments.

Because the focus is on the culture, we are not here concerned with individual behavior and individual desires. In the area of absenteeism, for example, we aren't concerned only with the level of absenteeism; we are also concerned with whether it is an acceptable behavior in the organization.

The language and focus on norms serves another purpose: It has been found that much more candid responses are forthcoming when individuals are asked to react to what their group is doing, rather than what they themselves are doing. This is conducive to a more accurate diagnosis, and later on in the change process the material will be useful in helping people to focus on changing the norms of their group, rather than placing blame on individuals. For example, it is more effective to say, "What things can we do around here to support the confrontation of absenteeism?" than to place blame, thereby putting the individual on the defensive for not confronting it.

Preliminary to Using the Norm Indicator

Before the decision is made about whether to use the existing norm indicator or to construct a variation for a particular project, some preliminary steps need to be taken. First, a brief narrative description of the "ideal" or "desired" organizational culture can be devised. Discussions involving key concerned people from all levels of the organization will revolve around the kind of environment people would find most satisfying and most effective in accomplishing the organization's objectives. Then there should be a consideration of the normative characteristics of such an ideal organization, with attention to pinpointing which norms would help develop and maintain it and which norms would interfere. These normative statements can then be used in checking through the basic norm indicator to see how well it suits the particular project, or they can be used in the construction of a new variation of the basic indicator. This procedure was followed, for example, in the development of an indicator for an Israeli kibbutz. Preliminary discussions revolved around the ideal that people envisioned, and there was discussion about the positive and negative norms that people observed in day-to-day living. Areas of particular concern that needed greater emphasis were added to the norm influence areas of the basic indicator.

Birth of a Norm Indicator

Statements, or items of the basic norm indicator, were developed through a step-by-step procedure that began with an initial meeting with various groups throughout the organization, in which the opening question raised was, "What norms make up a successful organization?" The first group of statements was added to and modified in subsequent meetings, with people of all levels having an input.

When variations of the norm indicator are tailor-made for a particular project, the opening question might have to do with a special concern of the organization. For example, in a recent tailor-made indicator, the opening question had to do with norms involved in the chronic hostility between the marketing and production divisions of the company. "What would be happening between the divisions if things were going well?" was the initial question.

Administering the Instrument

The norm indicator is essentially self-administered. It can be completed by individuals, either alone or in a group, or it can be completed as a group exercise. Since the statements are simple and precise observations of behavior, the indicator can be used at all levels of an organization.

The norm indicator is primarily designed as a pencil-and-paper instrument. When it is administered in this way, a question booklet and separate answer sheet are provided, together with forms for completing norm profiles (goal-setting instruments, to be described later in this chapter). Where reading skills are a problem, tape recordings or individual face-to-face administration can be arranged.

Specific directions for completing the instrument are provided in the question booklet. In addition, the administrator is usually available to make sure participants fully understand the directions and response categories. It is important that they be clear as to the reference groups in question. It is usually helpful for the administrator to interpret what "around here" means (i.e., work team, department, or total organization) and to be sure the participants have this group in mind when completing the instrument.

Scoring

The norm indicator is self-scoring and can be either hand-scored by a tabulator or centrally scored and interpreted. Forms and directions for hand-scoring are provided for both individual and group responses. When group responses are hand-scored, a two-part process is involved, calling for the tallying of individual responses on a scoring form and the graphing of frequency percentages for the group to make up norm profiles.

VARIATIONS OF
THE NORM INDICATOR

The categories used in a norm indicator will vary according to the project. It is important to be continually responsive to the needs of the particular organizational culture under study, and care must be taken that instruments, even the most useful ones, do not become dogmatic authorities, but remain flexible tools, able to bend to new situations. Organizations have been able to take the basic indicator and, reviewing the categories therein, select those areas that match their particular concerns. Sometimes they have adapted the basic indicator, other times they have started anew, building a new indicator around a particular problem but retaining the essential features of the original insofar as language, form, and scoring are concerned.

Indicators for
Special Purposes

Currently, complete norm indicators are available in the following variations:

- Basic Norm Indicator for Organizations
- Family Norm Indicator
- Leadership Norm Indicator

- Norm Indicator for College and University Classes
- Litter Culture Indicator for Communities
- Norm Indicator for Unions
- Health Practice Norm Indicator (101 Negative Norms)
- Norm Indicator for a Kibbutz Culture
- Norm Indicator on Quality Control
- Norm Indicator on Absenteeism
- Norm Indicator on Productivity
- Mental Health Culture Norm Indicator for Communities
- Norm Indicator on Organizational Teamwork
- Norm Indicator for Small Groups

Norms Diagnostic Index

Another variation of particular interest to businesses is the Norms Diagnostic Index (NDI). Through a combination of factor analysis and pragmatic judgmental techniques, the original pool of eighty-four survey items used in the norm indicator was reduced to a final set of thirty-eight statements dealing directly with organizational norms in seven primary areas. To this was added an additional set of thirteen items covering pay, communications, the work itself, and benefits. These items were included in order to provide in a single instrument both a comprehensive analysis of an organization's norms and a measure of popular job satisfaction dimensions. In a correlation study, NDI factors were compared with the Job Descriptive Index (P. C. Smith, et al.). High correlations were noted between the NDI's "supportive climate" and the JDI's "work and people" factors—a reflection of the profound importance of the emotional component of daily working experience.[2]

The Norm Profile

By combining responses within the various norm influence categories into a total response pattern, it is possible to trace a norm profile that graphically shows the "features" of the organization. Every cultural group has its own normative pattern. Like fingerprints, no two organizational profiles are exactly alike. Figures 3 and 4 show norm profiles for organizations. Note that the catego-

[2]Robert F. Allen and Frank Dyer, "A Tool for Tapping the Organizational Unconscious," *Personnel Journal*, 55, no.2 (March 1980), 192–198.

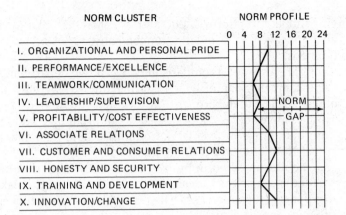

Figure 3. Norm Profile of a Troubled Company. (Copyright 1968 by HRI)

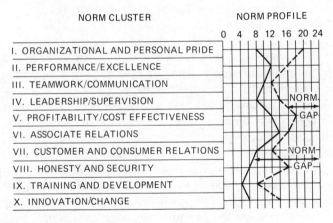

Figure 4. Comparison of Two Norm Profiles. (Copyright 1968 by HRI)

ries of influence areas as well are shaped by the needs of the particular company.

In the first profile, we see that the company was burdened with negative norms in the areas of Teamwork/Communication, Profitability/Cost Effectiveness, and Training and Development. At the time the profile was taken, the company, saddled with an old-line management philosophy, was rapidly headed toward bankruptcy. The low norm areas were chosen for immediate focus, bringing hope for improvement and a belief that change was possible and eventually pulling the company out of its financial predicament.

In figure 4 we see a comparison between two departments in the same company, one of which is achieving better results than the other. While the department on the right (the dotted line) is achieving relative success, it nonetheless can profit by working on its norms in the areas of Teamwork/Communication, Customer and Consumer Relations, and Training and Development.

As the illustrated norm profiles indicate, the ideal or desired norm patterns can be easily designated on the same graph, making readily apparent the differences between a group's perception of its potentialities and its actualities.

The norm profile is essentially a deficiency scale, measuring the "real" against the "ideal." This has both advantages and disadvantages, as compared with a scale based on an industry-wide mean, as some people advocate.

The deficiency scale offers the advantage of showing people the gap between what they really want and what they have, which might be quite different from a gap between what they have and what other similar organizations have. Some managers would consider it more useful to compare the company with the rest of the industry—in terms of salary, for example, school managers would find it unnecessary to raise salaries to an "ideal" level if the other school districts were comparable to theirs.

Another interesting way of illustrating the ideal is to show the span of the score, the standard deviation around a mean. When the span is larger, it might indicate some subgroups. For example, if the span is wide on the category of Communication, it might be that older employees are not troubled by a lack of communication but that newer employees are feeling left out. Or there might be groupings by sex or by educational level or a difference between salaried and hourly employees. Because of these differences in subgroups, the norm profile is probably most meaningful with small groups of about ten.

Nonetheless, the norm profile has proved to be a useful device in getting a group to see visually the critical areas of concern, and in helping it focus on them.

USES OF "AS I SEE IT..."
AND THE SUPPORT BAROMETER

These two instruments can be used during all four phases of the cultural change process. First, they are helpful in diagnosis and objectives setting. During the introduction of the program, they are teaching instruments. Later they help to focus implementation on the proper areas. And finally they are evaluation and renewal tools. Let us look at the various ways in which they can contribute at various stages of the change process that was described in chapter 2.

AS DIAGNOSTIC TOOLS.

The norm indicator "As I See It..." and the support barometer can be used in the analysis of any size group or organization, including large corporations where thousands of employees can have an input into the change process. They can be used by any type of group—business, educational, government, community, institutional, and so on. Even stranger groups can use them. Last year, for example, a stranger group met to examine their health practices and used the Health Practices Norm Indicator to diagnose their awareness of cultural influences upon their individual health habits and behaviors. In contrast, a large multilevel corporation undertaking a total company development effort has used "As I See It...," a norm indicator for organizations, to involve each one of its 987 employees in the diagnosis of organizational problems.

AS AIDS TO OBJECTIVE SETTING.

The norm profile that evolves in the interpretation of norm indicator scores is an easily read picture of the gap between what people want and what is actually happening. Discussions of this gap help people to set objectives that are specific enough to lead to meaningful tasks that will instill the changes necessary for success.

AS TEACHING TOOLS.

Both the support barometer and the "As I See It..." are useful as teaching tools in the early stages of a culture change project. By using these instruments, people get a feel for dealing with norms, a sense of how powerful cultural influences are in their lives, and an awareness of alternatives that are open to them.

AS IMPLEMENTATION TOOLS.

The importance of having a good flow of relevant information during the execution of tasks underscores the value of having an efficient monitoring device. Through the reapplication of the instruments or parts of them as necessary, measurement of the results can be achieved easily, and thus the flow of cultural information can be kept accurate and current. Feedback involving these results, at intervals during the execution of the project tasks, acts as a motivating force for further actions. When the norm indicator shows, for example, that it is the norm around the organization for people to be enthusiastic and turned on about their jobs, that will be an indication that there is wide support and acceptance of that kind of behavior and will encourage further progress.

FOR MEANINGFUL EVALUATION
AND RENEWAL.

Once a development effort is implemented, the readministration of these instruments is one important factor in evaluating progress and in determining if the process is indeed complete, rather than just superficial. Many companies have used them a year after the project completion to check on the holding power of the changes made and to renew and strengthen positive norms. The instruments are helpful as a way of ensuring that the progress will be maintained and that problems will be diagnosed early. They are also helpful in deciding on new areas to work on and in establishing new improvement goals. Since the instruments are open-ended, new items and categories can be added to provide information in specific new areas of concern that might arise.

There are problems in using any attitude survey for evaluation. Over periods of time, changes in personnel, policies, and outside factors might have effects that make for attitude changes, and this makes it difficult sometimes to see what can be attributed to the interventions of the change program. However, the indicators have been found to be reliable, certainly recording more permanent than transient perceptions—and people have been found to respond consistently over a lapse of several weeks in tested situations. Further testing will be necessary to gauge their reliability as evaluators in interventions over long periods of time. Certainly they have been found to be extremely useful in rediagnosing an organization after a year or two or even more, to see what kind of problems are currently in need of attention. Many companies have used an indicator a year after the completion of a project to check on the holding power of the new norms and to renew and strengthen them.

In summary, these are tools that, by themselves, don't change people, but that can be very helpful in the context of a total cultural change program.

II
BUILDING SUPPORTIVE ENVIRONMENTS

chapter five

The Open Organization

Change programs in organizations are usually undertaken with a lot of attention to such factors as management style, interdepartmental communication, information flow, and so on, all of which can be important. However, the greatest single factor that can help a change effort succeed and maintain that success is often overlooked. This is the development of a *sense of community and openness* among members of the group, with an emphasis on sharing, caring, building trust, and being open to one another.

When an organization or group undertakes a task without this (whether the task has to do with productivity, absenteeism, juvenile delinquency, litter, health promotion, or whatever), there may be short-term success. But unless the group creates a supportive environment, their achievements will have little likelihood of being maintained over the long run.

NORMS OF AN OPEN ORGANIZATION

Being "open" means making ourselves conscious of destructive patterns and then giving human interests a high priority, but group interests an equally high priority. In an open organization, we perceive to be operating such norms as the following:

- People work well together.
- People backstop each other.
- People see each other as people (not as objects or a pair of hands).
- People are supportive of one another.
- People have trust and confidence in one another.
- People don't have to protect their egos.
- When people have a problem with a program, they seek out the person who can do something about it.
- People recognize each other's contributions.
- People are free in their praise of one another.
- People can let their co-workers know when they are upset.
- People have a "sense of community"—what happens to others in the group and to the organization as a whole is important to them.
- People handle problems openly and constructively.

WHY "COMMUNITY" IS SO OFTEN OVERLOOKED

If the sense of community is so helpful, we might well ask why it is so difficult to achieve. The problem has its roots in the cultures that we have grown up in, as well as in those that we live in today.

In a sense we are "born free" but are immediately caught in the traps our cultures set up for us. One of the biggest of these is the extreme focus on individuality that we find in Western cultures. We are taught from our early years to see problems as individual problems and to seek individual solutions. We are exhorted to "pull ourselves up by our own bootstraps" and to "do our own thing." "Self-reliance" is a prime virtue, and the more we can do for ourselves by ourselves, the more approval we get from society. If this were true individuality, and if it were counterbalanced by an equal appreciation of group problems, group-reliance, and group solutions, all would be fine. But we tend to ignore cultural considerations—and teach our children to ignore them by our example. Fearing to lose our individuality and our human rights, we actually stunt our individuality and cut down on our alternatives. Individuality that separates us from other human beings eventually increases rather than reduces conformity.

These cultural proclivities are buttressed by some deep human needs. The drive *for* community comes from our social need—particularly our need to interact with other humans. The drive *against* it comes from a conflicting and equally powerful one—the need to be different. This, in the eyes of mathematician/historian Jacob Bronowski, is the human dilemma: Man, the "social solitaire," starts life with a long-dependent childhood, and the need for social connectedness remains for the rest of our lives; conversely, each person is alone, conscious of his or her individuality and separateness.

Each side of our dual nature has its purpose: Without others, we couldn't survive; without the desire to be unique, we would not have human rights, individual freedom, and personal and spiritual growth. Born out of reactions to conformity, restraint, oppression, and authoritarianism, the struggle for individual autonomy has brought humankind a long way.

We don't want to go back to the conformity of extreme nationalism or to the conflict of religious fanaticism, and we certainly don't want to give up what we have achieved in individual rights.

Our problem is that we want relationships and connectedness, but we don't want to lose individuality. The two needs, however, are not really mutually exclusive, even though we often treat them that way. In fact, they are mutually interdependent. If relationships in a group are based on respect for each person's right to fulfill his or her own potential, then both the need for relatedness and the need to be a unique individual are fulfilled. As we pointed out in chapter 1, the best way to satisfy both individual goals and group needs is to see ourselves as part of our cultures, contributing to and being influenced by cultural norms.

DISCOVERING
YOUR GROUP'S
NONSUPPORTIVE NORMS

It is evident that the norms we want become more attainable when they are seen as norms created by the group. This is particularly true of norms related to a "sense of community," which is so important to the successful implementation of change programs. Unfortunately, many of our organizations and institutions are replete with nonsupportive norms that prevent a sense of community from developing.

By taking the brief test below, you can get an indication of the extent of negative, nonsupportive norms that are influencing your organization.

A Brief Test of Nonsupportive Norms

How much are you plagued by the nonsupportive norms of the groups to which you belong? How much are these negative norms affecting you and your organization, family, business, or school? Try rating your environment, applying the statements below to any group that is important to you. Remember, a norm is not an individual behavior or habit, but rather the behavior that is expected, supported, and accepted by the group.

Around here, it is the norm for people to

- point out problems and mistakes much more frequently than they do strengths or accomplishments
- depend on others to make decisions for them
- not take the time to get to know one another
- admire the person who "keeps cool" and doesn't display emotions
- treat people not as whole human beings, but rather as "a pair of hands" for accomplishing organizational goals.
- have some level of distrust for one another
- feel they can't change things
- feel alienated from one another
- let others take the responsibility for solving crucial problems
- feel others have the power
- hang onto the old ways of doing things even when times change
- let red tape get in the way of their effectiveness
- expect people to "go along" without questioning
- act as though the organization, institution, or group is more important than the people in it
- not really listen to one another's ideas

The most valuable thing about this exercise is not the score but the recognition of supportive and nonsupportive norms for you and your group. If a sense of community is an important value in your organization, the negative norms will need to be understood, identified, and changed.

PUTTING PERSONAL AND GROUP INTERESTS TOGETHER

"I'm afraid I'll get lost in the group." "I'd rather do it myself." "It's more manly to handle your problems by yourself, rather than cry for help." "I must find and rely on my own inner strength."

Statements like these are indicative of an underlying question: How can we hold on to our individuality in a group-focused project?

We tend to think we have to make a choice of either strengthening ourselves or strengthening the group. Our present Western preoccupation with finding "the self" and centering upon our own inner needs has led us to downplay the strength we can get from the group. But we do not have to make an either/or choice here. We can help ourselves by helping the group, and vice versa. By building up the strength of one, we build up the strength of the other.

The more "centered" and self-fulfilled we are, the more we are able to reach out and care for others. This is something people are beginning to see more clearly. But the opposite—that the more we strengthen the group and care for others, the more we are offering our individuality a boost—is still largely a hidden area in our culture. What we feel is that we are sacrificing ourselves to help the group, but this is not so. We help ourselves as individuals when we help create positive group norms that reinforce and support us.

It can be helpful to show people a grid like the one in figure 5. It demonstrates graphically individual interests and group interests working together simultaneously. Put your group's "special interest" on the line marked "Cultural Aims."

Ask some members of your organization: How would you rate your organization? Where on the grid would you place the kind of group effort you are achieving? If there is a primary concern for individual needs, it would rate a 9-1. If there is a primary concern for the group, it would find itself on the 1-9 spot, where the individual is insignificant. We aren't likely to find such

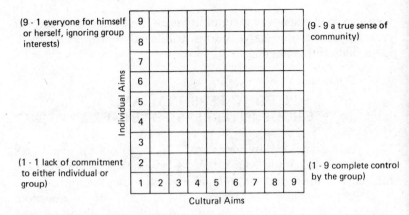

(9 - 1 everyone for himself or herself, ignoring group interests)

(9 - 9 a true sense of community)

(1 - 1 lack of commitment to either individual or group)

(1 - 9 complete control by the group)

Individual Aims

Cultural Aims

Figure 5. Individual/Culture Grid.

extremes; most of us find that our groups are somewhere in between, a 5-2 or a 4-7 perhaps. Since there is a tendency in the Western world to place greater emphasis on the individual, many groups would fall within that area. The chief purpose of the grid, however, is not to determine accurately where you might find yourself and your group, but to open people up to the idea of working toward the ideal—the 9-9 position where individual and group efforts are both strong, enhancing each other.

Use of grids such as these can help people get past the feeling that competitive, win-lose situations are necessary and inevitable, and see that it is possible to work together for win-win solutions from which everyone will benefit.

The important things to be concerned with on both individual and group levels are taking responsibility for what happens and working openly and trustingly with a support group. Rather than leaving decisions up to "the company," the professional, the experts "out there," we need to see ourselves as partners with them, using their expertise and resources without handing over the ultimate decision making to them.

In workshops we use topics such as the following to spark sharing experiences:

- A short personal history that highlights key personal experiences.
- "Some of the things in my life that are most important to me"
- "Some people or events that have had a significant impact on the way I am today"

- "An important success that I have had or a problem that I have managed to overcome"
- "One of the most important things that has happened to me in the past year"
- "Some things I really enjoy doing"

Other ways to generate sharing experiences are suggested in the following list:

A MULTIDIMENSIONAL
SHARING EXPERIENCE

Some possible topics to use:

- a brief impressionistic history of some of the more important things that have happened in your life.
- a person who has had an important impact on you and your life
- how you happened to come to your present work
- an experience you have had in the last year or two that has had an important impact on you
- an obstacle you have had to overcome
- a success you have had
- your hobbies and/or special interests
- one thing about you that we would have to understand if we wanted to know you better
- a childhood experience that has had a lasting impact on you

EMPHASIS ON PROCESS

In developing an open organization, the process is as important as the goal. Though the goal is to achieve openness and a sense of community, it doesn't happen at the end of the effort—it has to start happening in the interactions of group members from the beginning. The means and ends must be compatible.

Sharing More of Ourselves

To begin with, we need to see ourselves as multidimensional people and share more dimensions of ourselves with others. In our organizations, communities, and other groups, we tend to present ourselves in a particular role—as consultant, or mayor, or supervisor, and so on—and hide other aspects of ourselves from our fellow workers and associates. The more we can share these other aspects, the more we build a sense of trust and positive support. There will always be parts of ourselves we do not want to share, and parts of ourselves we do not even consciously understand— but for most of us there is much beyond this that we can learn to share and use in building stronger relationships and a stronger sense of community.

Practicing Openness

The beginning of the opening-up process often happens for people in the workshop situation of Phase II, where they are first introduced to the culture change program that a company has undertaken. Here, in the comparative safety and protection of the workshop situation, they can begin to practice the new norms. Often this is easier for people to do in a workshop, away from the job location—and this can be very valuable so long as the new behavior is carried back into day-to-day behavior on the job. To accomplish this, it is necessary for most people to have an ongoing circle of support. As we will see in the next chapter, there are ways we can make use of the small groups we are part of to provide this support, or we can create special small groups for that purpose.

In order finally to achieve an open organization, we need to start by building norms of openness—and this beginning can be a commitment to the process, a process that starts when we are more open with the next person we meet.

A Guide
to Constructive Feedback

To build norms of openness, it is helpful to pay attention to the way we speak and act with one another, particularly the way in which we confront negative norms. These are bound to occur in force in the early stages of a change effort, and if not confronted, will probably continue. Therefore the way we give feedback to people is important.

To confront negative norms humanistically and to be able to offer constructive suggestions, certain guidelines for good feedback are helpful, and any organization development effort will benefit by spending some time reviewing them at one of its early meetings.

Feedback is helpful when it

- is intended to be constructive
- includes positive elements (not just negative ones)
- deals with issues people can do something about
- is specific and clear (avoiding generalities)
- is checked for communication (does the person receiving it get the point?)
- is checked for reliability (do others think the same about this topic?)
- leaves the person free to determine his or her own solutions and behavior
- is solicited, not imposed
- avoids emotion-laden words
- is given at an appropriate time[1]

Reinforcing with Rewards

One of the important contributions of behavioral science has been the research proving that rewarding certain behavior tends to reinforce it. Thus it is necessary and helpful not only to confront negative norms, but to reward the positive ones as they occur.

We can do this by acknowledging the positive gestures of openness and trust and sharing when they occur.

This seems a simple matter, yet how often do we reward competition between departments and ignore their cooperative efforts? How often do we let opportunities to praise people go by? How often, when we do get compliments, do we deny them instead of letting people know we appreciate the positive feedback?

We can reinforce our efforts to build openness by letting people know we appreciate it when they work well together, when they support each other, when they treat each other as human beings rather than objects.

---

[1]"Guidelines to Feedback" (Unpublished paper developed by the National Training Laboratories, 1958), p. 1.

chapter six
Building Support Through Small Groups

If our organizations and communities are going to change, the small subgroups within them will have to provide supportive environments for that change. The small groups of which we are members—our work groups, families, the classroom, the office staff, the board, the faculty, and so on—have a tremendous influence upon us. Each one of our primary groups (the people we actually associate with each day) is a small culture, full of norms that profoundly affect our lives. If our families smoke, we tend to smoke; if our friends drink, we are more likely to drink; if our co-workers support the distortion of expense accounts, we tend to distort ours; if the norm is to drive five miles over the speed limit, we tend to drive at that speed. Though every one of us has certain areas in which we confront or flaunt the norm, for the most part our lives are determined by the norms of our groups, especially our primary groups. Here the positive norms of community can have a great effect, and here, in the circle of associates around us every-day, is our best chance to develop that sense of community so vital to meaningful change.

YOU DON'T HAVE TO CHANGE THE WORLD

We have to be careful that people don't misunderstand when we talk in terms of culture and environment. To change the culture, or change the environment, sounds like a big order. But cultures are both large and small, and you don't have to start with the whole outer culture. You can start with the small groups that are part of your daily life.

We first began to realize the importance of the small group when we were working with delinquent youngsters in the inner city. We found that a small newly formed group could set its own positive norms, and by adding people slowly and helping them to understand themselves in a cultural context, a small supportive environment was built. This group—never more than fourteen teenage boys—gave the boys the support they needed to turn from their delinquent ways and carve new and better life-styles for themselves.[1]

Later, the same principle of creating small, positive subcultures was used in successful cultural change programs with migrant workers,[2] communities, families, agencies, unions, churches, and businesses.[3] Without waiting for the whole company to change, or for the whole community to be more humanistic, the subgroups can get the process going. Today this principle is proving useful in building successful corporate and community health programs. Here people who are trying to change to healthier life-styles find support in the small group. The sense of community that builds in such a group helps people more than education or factual knowledge about the value of health practices.[4]

Power in the Primary Group

The face-to-face group is such a powerful tool because it relates to a profound need in our lives. Robert Nisbet, in his book *The Quest for Community*, asks where we can find relief from the sense of isolation and anxiety that haunts us in our age of abundance, and answers that relief lies "in the realm of the small, primary, personal relationships of society—the relationships that mediate directly

[1]Robert F. Allen, Harry N. Dubin, Saul Pilnick, and Adella Youtz, *Collegefields: From Delinquency to Freedom* (Seattle: Special Child Publications, 1970).
[2]Sara Harris and Robert F. Allen, *The Quiet Revolution* (New York: Rawson-Wade, 1978).
[3]Robert F. Allen with Charlotte Kraft, *Beat the System: A Way to Create More Human Environments* (New York: McGraw-Hill, 1980).
[4]Robert F. Allen with Shirley Linde, *Lifegain* (Appleton-Century-Crofts, 1981).

between man and his larger world of economic, moral, and political and religious values."[5]

Small support groups create an opportunity for primary relationships to develop. We can learn to share with and trust one another within a group that is small enough for everyone to be heard, for everyone to get to know one another. Here the norms of "community" can be built and tried out, slowly and solidly. There is an opportunity to check back on these norms from time to time, to confront the negative norms when they creep back in, but confront them in a friendly, trusting way.

A support group, when properly developed, can become the very opposite of the closed "clique," for it radiates outward, often building norms of community strong enough to make it possible for its members to practice the positive behaviors not only in the group but in the outer world as well.

TYPES OF SUPPORT GROUPS

There are many types of support groups. They include small groups already set up for other purposes—such as boards, class-rooms, committees, work groups, small departments—which can be transformed into supportive environments for their members. While such groups would continue to devote their major effort to the tasks for which they were set up, they would also put aside time to view themselves as a culture, look at the kind of support they are giving to their members, and work to develop more of the kind of norms that they want. In a change program, time set aside for this has proved valuable and worthwhile. Too often in installing change programs, people tend to be like the proverbial woodcutter who is too busy to sharpen his ax, with the result that he gets further and further behind. In terms of solving chronic problems or accomplishing meaningful and lasting change, time will be saved in the long run if we first spend some ax-sharpening time on developing support. When we tried this in a classroom situation, for instance, devoting the first few weeks of school in the fall to building the classroom into a supportive environment for learning,

[5]Robert Nisbet, *The Quest for Community* (New York: Oxford University Press, 1953), pp. 48–49.

it resulted in a much more smoothly running classroom the rest of the year, one in which students were able to help each other in a remarkably cooperative atmosphere. Furthermore, they agreed that the learning experience was much more fun!

In corporate settings, similar phenomena have been observed. A large retail company involved in an organization-wide cultural change program found out just how valuable the support group idea can be. Work groups already set up were helped to start the process of building good "community" norms. They quickly became support groups, creating the environment needed for sustained change. Within the first few months of the program the difference was already remarkable. Even customers coming in to the various stores felt it: The stores were becoming places where customers felt that their needs were important. The norms of caring had already begun to take effect.

GETTING STARTED

Essentially, supportive environments grow from the inside out. One person can have the idea and can start to put it into practice with one other. It is exciting to see how one person, armed with an idea, can become the change agent and start a process that can eventually spread through a whole organization.

Growing from the inside out does not mean a disregard for the powerful influence of the top level of management in the large hierarchical-type of organization. It is extremely helpful for the leaders to commit themselves publicly to the idea of developing "community" and thereby help to set up the climatic conditions that will aid its growth. However, the actual work of building a supportive environment is done on a person-to-person level, and the small support group is a powerful tool for making it happen.

You can start with small groups that already exist or you can consciously and purposefully create a new group. It can be a small group; in fact, you can start with as few as one or two other people. It might be a friend with whom you are sharing your concerns. It might be your husband or wife, or your whole family. It might be your business partner, or the people you work with in the office, or the whole department. Whoever it is, you have made a start when you first say to this person, "Let's talk about ways in which we can do things even better around here, ways in which we all can relate with more openness, ways we can take care of each other and our whole group's needs."

By your action you are already starting to develop a small subculture with different norms—norms of openness and caring. As you gradually add other people to your group, they can partake in the cooperative atmosphere you have created. Just getting a group together to achieve a common goal is not enough. There needs also to be a conscious effort to build good relationships among the people in the group, and to develop the supportive cultures that will undergird the task-oriented work of the group.

Quality Circles

The Japanese, borrowing a leaf from American OD technology, have recently begun to use what they call quality circles to give people from various jobs and job levels within an organization an opportunity to come together to contribute ideas for improved quality. As might be expected, the spirit as well as the ideas that are generated have been extremely useful. In our culture change programs in the United States, for more than twenty years we have been using a similar technique, which we now call QPT. QPT in this case stands for Quality, Production, and Teamwork. When supported on a continual basis by a reinforcing culture, such groups can make highly important contributions.

The support group approach is primarily one of democratic, participatory decision making and involvement. It is essentially self-led, though in some cases a support group leader, an organizational development practitioner, a chairperson, or a teacher may fulfill the leadership role. Whoever this person is, he or she is primarily a facilitator and coordinator rather than a director. Decisions about what will be discussed and which skills will be learned rest with the group as a whole, although groups can often benefit from the experiences of others.

Joining a support group is most often a voluntary action, and using some of the time of an ongoing group—such as a board or a classroom—for support group activities should be, to the extent possible, a group decision and not one imposed on it.

Ordinarily "small groups" means not more than twelve people. In the classroom situation, which in our case sometimes involved classes of thirty or more, the classroom was subdivided part of the time into groups of eight to twelve. In large corporations we often start with the executive committee of less than twelve people, then work with whole departments that report to members of the executive committee. The departments are subdivided into small groups after the initial workshop.

SOME WAYS TO HELP
SMALL GROUPS SUCCEED

Go from Special Interest
to Human Interest

Whatever your reason for starting the group—to solve a civic problem, to start a new business, to promote good health practices, to reduce absenteeism—make sure that the personal and human factors are not neglected by

- giving people a chance to get to know one another as people beyond the framework of the particular task or purpose
- giving each person in the group a chance to share feelings about the kind of support and encouragement he or she gets—and wants to get—from the group

Help People Understand
and Work with Cultural Norms

Often it is not too difficult for small groups to make a change, but the problem is maintaining it. People often start a project with great enthusiasm and cooperation, but the old norms take over and the group spirit evaporates when someone is left with the work or someone finds emotional needs unsatisfied. We Americans especially find it easy to latch onto fads, to grasp at a novel idea and adopt it quickly—and then just as quickly drop it and go back to the old way of doing things. We jog awhile, diet awhile, meditate awhile—and then go back to our more sedentary, weightier, more stressful ways.

In the small group you can help people become aware of typical norms of handling change. The more we can be conscious of these norms and how they operate in our lives, the better we will be able to keep a firm hand on them and circumvent their destructive influence.

It Doesn't Have to
Take a Lot of Time

Small group meetings can be short and simple. We know of some section leaders who get together for a meeting after lunch every Monday. It is a simple matter of reporting quickly any new achievement or obstacles. The meeting is not task-oriented, and it is not used for solving large problems. It is time set aside for sharing concerns and celebrating successes. It is a time to check in with each other on how they are doing. The important work of changing behavior is taking place in day-to-day activities. "We live the OD program every day," is the slogan of one change program. The small group is the place to check to see how the day-to-day changes are doing, and how people feel about them, and it is the place to go to evaluate progress.

Include the Leaders

Many times work groups create support groups but exclude the supervisors and organizational leaders. It is our judgment that in hierarchical organizations it is better to include the leaders. The argument is sometimes given that members will not feel free to speak when the leaders are there. This feeling in itself is something that should be dealt with, and dealing with it face to face in a supportive environment is the most beneficial way to solve the problem.

Don't Be Exclusive

The difference between a small supportive group and a clique is openness. To be open means not only to be supportive of each other within the group but to be open to others who are without. Openness is a way of being. Most of us can better maintain changes in ourselves and in our groups by reaching out to be helpful to other people.

Focus on Small-Group Norms

By focusing on norms, one can avoid blame placing and finger pointing. The norm indicator designed especially for small groups can be used as a teaching tool for people to learn about norms. It includes both positive and negative norm statements like the following:

Some Key Norms
for Small Groups to Consider
It's a norm around here for the group and/or its members . . .

1. to confuse freedom with license.
2. to accept responsibility for their own behavior and for the impact that their behavior has upon others.
3. to feel that their right to freedom makes it unfair for others to react negatively to their behavior in any way.
4. to have rigid expectations for each other's behavior.
5. to expect and even encourage a wide range of member differences.
6. to stress and encourage conformity in their relationships with one another.
7. to be sure that the exercise of their individual freedom doesn't interfere with the freedom of others.
8. to view member freedom as an essential component of group life.
9. to participate fully in the work of the group.
10. to make sure that each member of the group has an opportunity to become fully involved.
11. to make sure that each member feels free to contribute ideas and suggestions.
12. to strike an effective balance between individual freedom and group responsibility.
13. to solicit and encourage feedback as to how the exercise of their freedom is affecting the group and its members.
14. to assume responsibility for the success of the group.
15. to assume responsibility for their own performance.
16. to let others assume responsibility for the effectiveness of the group.
17. to feel deeply involved in the meetings of the group.

18. to show a very low concern for the success of the group.
19. to assume responsibility for their own preparation for group meetings.
20. to stress excellence in all important group activities.
21. to be satisfied with low levels of individual and group performance.
22. not to be satisfied with less than outstanding performance.
23. to be continually on the lookout for better and more effective ways of doing things.
24. not to care about the level of the group's performance.
25. to be satisfied with mediocre ways of doing things.
26. to take pride in the group and in the group's accomplishments.
27. to show little pride in the group or its work.
28. to take pride in their own work and in the work of the group.
29. to make sure that all group members have a clear understanding of and commitment to group goals.
30. to proceed in group activities without people having a clear idea of the goals or procedures that have been established.
31. to understand and be committed to the goals of the group.
32. to go along with group activities without understanding the problem.
33. to relate discussion and action to group goals.
34. to be impatient with members who want clarification or have questions about the group direction.
35. to focus on the achievement of the goals that the group has set for itself.
36. to measure progress toward goals regularly.
37. to make effective use of available time.
38. to take up group time with irrelevant matters.
39. to point out better ways to use or save time.
40. to show they aren't concerned about the group's time by arriving late, leaving early, or wasting time.
41. to make sure that leadership is a responsibility that is shouldered by all the group members.
42. to avoid the responsibilities of leadership.
43. to assign leadership on the basis of who can be "drafted" for the job, rather than on the basis of who would be best for the assignment.
44. to accept responsibility for meeting the leadership needs of the group.
45. to model the behavior that is expected of other group members.
46. to expect the leader to take sole responsibility for the success of the group.

47. to make sure that the leadership needs of the group are being met.
48. to emphasize the importance of leadership skills.
49. to select and use the most appropriate methods and procedures for a given task.
50. to use group methods and procedures that are unrealistic, outdated, or unrelated to the needs of the group.
51. to regularly discuss changes in methods or procedures that might help the group to accomplish its goals.
52. to feel they have to work around existing methods and procedures in order to get anything done.
53. to stick with the same set methods and procedures even when they are inappropriate.
54. to make the best use of the team resources that are available to them.
55. to overlook opportunities for the better use of team resources.
56. to practice effective teamwork.
57. to stress the importance of effective teamwork.
58. to work well and effectively with one another.
59. to show little interest in building effective teamwork with the group.
60. to be working at cross-purposes with one another.
61. to allow subgroup antagonisms to dominate the climate of the group.
62. to emphasize cooperation over individual accomplishment.
63. to confront negative norms and negative behavior constructively.
64. to provide recognition and support to group members for their contributions to the group.
65. to provide recognition and support for positive behavior within the group.
66. to point out errors in a way that is constructive and helpful.
67. to fail to confront negative behavior consistently, even when it gets in the way of the group's functioning.
68. to give at least equal attention to group successes as it does to group failures.
69. to focus continually on the group's failures and shortcomings.
70. to build a positive success orientation within the group.
71. to express pride and satisfaction in the group and its work.
72. to be continually focused on the shortcomings of the group **and** seldom on its strengths and achievements.
73. to look for ways of assuring the group's success rather than complaining about its failures.
74. to treat each other with dignity and respect.
75. to be concerned with the well-being of each group member.
76. to be supportive of one another.

77. to show little concern for the development of positive human relationships.
78. to allow individual antagonisms to dominate the climate of the group.
79. to allow manipulation and strategy to become the means of accomplishing group business.
80. to get to know each other as people rather than group members.
81. to give group members constructive help when they are having difficulty.
82. to give and receive feedback in constructive ways.
83. to give feedback that is mostly negative or destructive.
84. to level with each other about their feelings and opinions in constructive ways.
85. to be visibly open and trusting in each other in all the actions of the group.
86. to build a spirit of mutual trust and openness with one another.
87. to be distrustful and closed off from one another.
88. to push problems under the rug rather than to get them out in the open so that they can be dealt with promptly and constructively.
89. to complain about problems rather than do something about them.
90. to make sure that the quality of the decision made by the group is the best possible.
91. to make sure that group members are fully involved in decisions affecting them.
92. to put people down rather than seek to solve the problems that bother them.
93. to neglect the involvement of people in the decision-making process.
94. to show little concern for the quality of the decisions made by the group.
95. to substitute blame placing and complaining for problem solving.
96. to handle problems or differences in a way that is constructive rather than damaging or divisive.
97. to feel that conflicts are natural in any group and should be handled openly.
98. to avoid making decisions and allow group problems to become chronic.
99. to seek out the ideas and opinions of others actively.
100. to listen carefully to one another.
101. to be so interested in communicating their own ideas that they pay little attention to the ideas of others.
102. to focus on communication as a two-way rather than a one-way process.

103. to check consistently as to whether they are being understood and whether they are understanding what others are saying.
104. to have a strong commitment to arriving at the best decisions.
105. not to laugh at one another when someone makes a mistake.
106. to explain their ideas clearly and to check to see if they are understood.
107. to be concerned with the growth and development of each group member.
108. to handle mistakes or misunderstandings in such a way as to encourage member growth.
109. to put people down as opposed to trying to help them.
110. to provide feedback to one another as to things that are being done well and things that need improvement.
111. to help individual members focus on their own individual goals as well as the goals of the group.
112. to see that any necessary orientation and training is provided for group members.
113. to be on the lookout for new and better ways of doing things.
114. to examine the work of the group regularly so that group functions can be improved.
115. to follow through on the change efforts that are begun.
116. to base change efforts on sound information and sound decision-making processes.
117. to avoid blame placing and instead look for constructive approaches to change.
118. to approach change by dealing with the real causes of problems and not just the symptoms.
119. to change things without consulting the people who would be affected by the change.
120. to approach change efforts systematically rather than haphazardly.

BUILDING A COMMUNITY WITHOUT WALLS

If supportive principles are at work in a small group within the larger organization, a positive culture can be built that can withstand the negative norms that may abound in the total organization. But even better yet is the spread of the positive norms outside the group where they originate. If people can avoid blame placing within their support group, they often find they can also avoid blame placing in the next department meeting or within their family situation.

If there are a number of support groups within the larger organization and they are developing good norms of relatedness and trust among their members, it is bound to affect the larger organization itself, and if the leadership of the organization has already committed itself on paper or in verbal commitment to seeking a greater sense of community, then the change can take place rapidly.

When people discover that their true individuality can grow within the group and that they need not fear manipulation and control when there is an open exchange between people, then the sense of community is able to spread rapidly. It cannot be contained within the "walls" of any particular group, since fortunately, it is one of our most contagious human traits.

chapter seven
The Leadership Role

Over the past few decades there has been a changing picture of what an effective organizational leader should be. In the early decades of this century, a leader was expected to exude willpower, diligence, self-confidence, personal ambition, and competitiveness. The "captain of industry" was authoritative and domineering, and business organizations were largely paternalistic. The manager's goal was high productivity and profits. He wanted to get the most work out of the people below him, and performance was what counted. This "Theory X" type of manager assumed that people were basically lazy and antiwork.[1] He had to hold a tight rein on the organization. Performance was what counted, and task completion was his main goal.

Then the "organization man" took his place, and the focus of decisions and responsibility was broadened to the group.

Many of the earlier trappings of Theory X leadership went slightly underground, and the ability to work with and through the people was not a prime requisite. Teamwork was a slogan, but as long as the leader remained captain of the team, an effort was made to keep people happy and contented, but not necessarily involved or making full use of their resources.

[1]Douglas McGregor, The Human Side of Enterprise (New York: McGraw-Hill, 1960).

Some people have suggested that the organization man gave way to a different kind of leader. According to this theory, upwardly mobile corporate executives today have a different goal—selling themselves. It is the impression that counts, not the performance itself or the completion of the task. The impression of success is what is important. Such leaders, moving from company to company, sell themselves. As Lasch says, "The successful bureaucrat survives not by appealing to the authority of his office but by establishing a pattern of upward movement, cultivating upwardly mobile superiors, and administering 'homeo-pathetic doses of humiliation' to those he leaves behind in his ascent."[2]

With this kind of leader, personal success does not depend on loyalty to the organization so much as on loyalty to developing a successful image of oneself. This is "the gamesman," as Maccoby labeled him, who manipulates others subtly—not in a domineering manner, as the captain of industry did, but nonetheless it is manipulation for the purpose of winning over others, or at least appearing to. "His main goal is to be known as a winner, and his deepest fear is to be labeled a loser."[3]

THE LEADER
AS CULTURAL CHANGE AGENT

From "captain of industry" to "organization man" to "gamesman," leadership styles often change with the times. We propose an even more basic shift in management style—the leader who doesn't direct the activities of others but rather works with others to accomplish shared objectives. An effective leader is someone who does things *with* people, not alone. This leader is not an authority figure or pseudo-father, but a cultural change agent.

The leader of tomorrow is thus a change agent who sees himself or herself as part of the organizational or community culture, not one who grasps for power but one who encourages the sharing of power; not a manipulator but one who helps people see clearly where they are and where they want to go; not a pusher but a facilitator and a participant who helps build enthusiasm and hope for changes that are chosen by the members of the culture.

[2]Christopher Lasch, *The Culture of Narcissism* (New York: W.W. Norton, 1979), p. 122.
[3]Michael Maccoby, *The Gamesman: The New Corporate Leaders* (New York: Simon and Schuster, 1976), p. 100.

We would like to propose that the very definition of successful leadership is the ability to bring about sustained culture change. After all, the leader who cannot do this contributes very little in the long run. The leader who only brings about short-term changes that evaporate quickly may even be doing a disservice to the organization. When people go through program after program that doesn't work or that works for a while and then collapses, the result is increased feelings of helplessness and frustration.

Use of the Cultural Change Process

Later on in this chapter we will be discussing a number of specific characteristics of the type of leader we are recommending. Before doing this we would like to talk about an overriding issue. The main difference between the new type of leader we are suggesting and those of the past is that the new leader uses an explicit process and sees that it is understood by others in the organization. If you hang onto the process you are using, it gives you power; if you share it with others, you also share the power. The new leader welcomes the opportunity to do this.

The earlier types of leaders tended to keep the process of leadership to themselves. The leaders we are suggesting share that process with others and hold the same rules for themselves as they do for others. Such leaders, for example, do not hold themselves immune to the need for cultural support, but own up to this need and find or create a support group for themselves.

The person who works with the cultural concept uses the four-phased process described in chapter 2 for both dealing with problems and achieving organizational goals and follows the principles described in the previous chapters, enumerating them so that others know these are the approved and supported rules of the game. The effective leader asks others to contribute to these rules, as well as to the overall process. When there is a chronic problem, this leader looks at it from the cultural perspective, using the principles to guide the organization in solving it.

Sharing Leadership with Others

The effective leader is one who sees leadership in terms of a function rather than in terms of a particular person. A group may need to have someone who chairs the meeting, someone who takes responsibility for seeing that an agenda is followed, someone who checks on the direction of the group or is responsible for convening and adjourning it. But this function can rotate from person to person.

Furthermore, responsibility for decision making can be broadly participatory, even in hierarchical organizations. Several years ago Harman International Industries in Tennessee tried an experiment wherein the basic unit for change consisted of small groups of workers and supervisors (often three and three). Through these discussion groups, the workers made decisions to rotate jobs, to supervise themselves, to work in teams, and to make other changes that improved the quality and satisfaction of their work life.

In Scandinavia, experiments in worker participation in management have been underway for a number of years, spurred on particularly by the work of Dr. Einar Thorsrud, a Norwegian social scientist. In England, E. F. Schumacher worked with a number of large organizations to create structures that required minimal administration.

In the United States, the Scott Bader Plastics Company was run by "a sort of parliament of workers, rather than by a board of directors. The workers could, in fact, choose or dismiss directors, and approve the salaries of chairman and directors."[4]

Experiments such as these show us some alternatives to the old idea of the leadership being vested in one man or one small group at the top. While we are not necessarily recommending that you imitate these approaches, we point them out as a way to open our minds to new and different possibilities. Some of the difficulties that befell many of these experiments might well have been avoided.

The New Participative Leader

Over the past decade there has been a great deal of talk about participative management. Unfortunately, there has been more confusion than clarity in actual practice. For some, participative management has meant an abdication of leadership responsibility.

[4]E. F. Schumacher, *Good Work* (New York: Harper and Row, 1979), p. 76.

For others, it has meant a choice between laissez-faire and authoritarian alternatives. In one organization we studied, leaders were told that participative management was the "in" thing to do, but were given little real help in developing the skills and techniques that were necessary to implement it.

The leadership continuum in figure 6 is based on one of the most helpful models for participative leadership, developed by Robert Tannenbaum and Warren Schmidt, which suggests that there is not just one skill for a participative leader but a number of skills in a continuum of leadership patterns.[5]

The skills appropriate to various points along the continuum range from making and announcing a decision to permitting non-managers to function within the limits defined by organizational restraints. (In early writings Tannenbaum and Schmidt used the words *subordinates* and *limits defined by superior* but later substituted *non-managers* and *organizational restraints*, as shown in figure 6.)

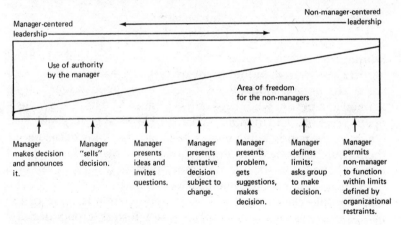

Figure 6. Continuum of Leadership Behavior.

One important characteristic of the effective participative leader is that he or she keeps people informed as to what role they are playing at a particular time. One of the greatest dangers in

[5]Robert Tannenbaum and Warren H. Schmidt, "How to Choose a Leadership Pattern," *Harvard Business Review*, 51, no. 3 (May–June 1973), 162–80. Reprinted with permission of the *Harvard Business Review*. Copyright © 1973 by the President and Fellows of Harvard College, all rights reserved.

applying participative leadership is that people's participation can become a sham rather than a reality. Nothing can turn people off more rapidly than being told that they are part of a decision-making process when in fact they are being manipulated into thinking they are. When the leader holds a meeting without making clear his or her intentions beforehand, participants can become very disappointed when they find the leader has gone on with predetermined decisions. Most members of organizations—particularly hierarchical ones—do not feel it is essential that they have an equal role in all decision-making processes. What they do desire is a greater clarity about their role. If a leader goes into a meeting with a decision already fairly well made, he or she would be well advised to share that view in the beginning, while hopefully at the same time listening to other viewpoints and staying open to change.

Characteristics
of an Effective Leader

Defining an effective leader probably depends a great deal on the particular organization, but there are certain positive qualities that cut across organizational lines. In general, a good leader can be defined as a person who helps others to succeed. His or her style is open, trusting, and nonmanipulative. He or she does not lead others by the hand, telling them what to do or making decisions for them, but helps them to explore problems, seek solutions, and install changes together. As a resource person, the leader can be a teacher, alerting people to new ideas and new materials, one who helps people clarify their tasks and goals, reminds them of the basic principles of cultural change, and fosters group decision making and group concensus when appropriate.

Today's new leaders are not gamespeople, but those who seek to expose games. If they play them at all, it is as openly as possible, with the intent not only to be aware that they are playing by arbitrarily selected rules, but to have others who are in the game with them see this also. These others do not therefore become competitors—people they must win over—and such leaders do not see themselves or others as either winners or losers.

Neither do these leaders see themselves as "servants of the people," but as on an equal level with the others, neither servant nor master. They are all part of a joint project and, even more important, they are partners in a higher ethic above exclusive loyalty to self, group, or organization.

In order not to be a manipulator—even a subtle type of manipulator who maintains a friendly posture and encourages "participation" while underhandedly pushing his or her will—the leader must be truly open to other people's ideas, must not intend to maneuver them, must not only be a listener but must foster group consensus as much as possible. It is difficult, particularly in our culture in which we have been taught to fake success in order to gain it, to rely on impressions and appearances rather than substance. It demands a stripping away of illusion about ourselves and our groups—the kind of ethical strength that unfortunately we have little training for.

There are a great many characteristics of effective leadership to consider. People have to relate them to their own personalities and situations. While it is probably impossible for any one person to embody all the characteristics of effective leadership at all times, there are certain ones, described in the following pages, that can be seen as models to work toward in an organization. All of these characteristics are much easier to develop if the organization's leadership norms are supportive.

LOOKS AHEAD POSITIVELY.

This leader is more interested in solutions and results than in exploring why things went wrong and affixing the blame. He or she finds no sense in wasting energy on past faults or searching out culprits, but instead spends energy in creating environments where there is no need for culprits or victims, where everyone is a winner.

IS ADDICTED TO CLARITY.

Clarity in all things is a value the new leader holds high. He or she wants to be sure that people understand tasks, goals, objectives, and job definitions, and keeps a constant check. This means being a good listener as well as a good communicator, staying sensitive to how things are coming across to others. It also means getting the precise information needed for the particular task, gathering sufficient data rather than going on hunches.

WORKS HARD
WITHOUT BEING A WORKAHOLIC.

Being a workaholic is not necessary for organizational success. If hard-working managers find themselves overburdened and feeling that they are the only ones keeping the company going, supporting the others, it would be wise to examine the involvement of others in the "ownership" of the project or the organization. Such managers might be acting as puppeteers, holding all the heavily weighted springs, when they need instead to be delegating tasks and authority to others.

EMPHASIZES BOTH
PEOPLE AND PRODUCTIVITY.

The effective leader will be concerned with both people and productivity and will not see them as conflicting. He or she will help others to see that the two factors are not incompatible and that they are, in fact, contributing to one another.

WORKS SYSTEMATICALLY,
USING A CULTURAL FRAMEWORK.

The effective leader will make sure of the four phases of the cultural change process (see chapter 2) in all aspects of his or her work. To begin with, the leader will work with others in analyzing the existing culture, setting objectives, and designing the change process. In designing the change process, effective approaches will be developed for introducing, implementing, and evaluating the program. The analysis will include a careful review of the various norm influence areas to determine how they can be modified and changed.

BUILDS A SUPPORTIVE COMMUNITY.

Effective leaders see themselves as part of the culture and a "life-space" that goes beyond the boundaries of the skin, consisting of both self and environment. Accepting themselves as part of the culture does not mean submitting to its tyranny, but working with others cooperatively to make cultural changes that will be good influences both on themselves and on the others of the group. Such leaders will build a support group for themselves, for leaders need their own support networks. This can usually be found with only a few people, sometimes a few members of the immediate staff. In addition, if there is need for greater skills of leadership, effective leaders find ways to acquire them. Some skill areas to be considered are performance planning and review, organizational policies and procedures, support and confrontation, effective work team meetings, communication and information systems, training, management-by-objectives, involving and motivating people, organizational problem solving, and orientation.

To test yourself on the characteristics of an effective leader of cultural change, you might consider the following list:

Characteristics of an Effective Leader
of Cultural Change: A Test You Can Give Yourself

1. Do you have a commitment to involve other people in the change process?
2. Do you share your vision with others and listen to their reactions?
3. Do you have a commitment to sustained change?
4. Do you let others know publicly about your commitment?
5. Are you concerned for both people and productivity issues and can you see that there is no conflict between the two?
6. Are you willing to share credit with others?
7. Do you care enough to confront people and problems in constructive ways?
8. Are you interested in further development of your own leadership skills?
9. Have you found or created a support group for yourself?
10. Do you try to create win-win solutions and avoid blame placing?
11. Are you willing to take the time to track results—cultural as well as performance and programmatic results?
12. Do you make use of the four-phased change process with all problems and programs?
13. Do you adhere to the principles of normative change?
14. Do you share yourself with others in a multidimensional way?
15. Do you take time to get a basis of sound information on which to base programs and decisions?

ARE LEADERS BORN OR MADE?

Too often we put people in leadership positions with no training in leadership. They may have had training in science, in the law, and so on, and, having done well, are rewarded with executive positions for which they have no training. People who are skilled as speakers, politicians, and so forth may be rewarded by being put into the position of mayor—or governor or college president—only to find they are called upon to use skills of leadership that they have never had an opportunity to develop.

When this happens, the skills can be developed. Nearly everyone has the capability of undertaking a leadership role and doing it well if given adequate skills and support. The Organizational Leadership Development Module System (OLDM), which we have used in diverse settings, has helped a variety of people improve their leadership skills (see appendix A).

THE "LIFE-SHARING" CONCEPT

Being an effective leader means presenting oneself in a multidimensional way to others of the group. It means sharing oneself as a total person, rather than presenting only a fragment—the part of the person who is "the CEO," "the manager," the "OD consultant," or "the expert" (see page 69).

Often consultants in the social sciences hold themselves apart, offering expertise as an OD specialist or efficiency expert, seeing themselves in only one dimension and not developing empathetic relationships with the people they are trying to help. They become mere observers of the culture they are dealing with, labeling people and categorizing them. In this way they themselves add to the separation of person from person, contributing to those anticommunity norms that plague our society. If they will see themselves as partners in the change effort rather than as experts dwelling outside of it, a great deal more can be done to improve the quality of the culture.

The same multidimensional approach applies to managers. Instead of allowing subordinates to see them only as "the boss," they need to present themselves as total persons, willing to share experiences and attitudes that lie outside their manager's role.

Life sharing does not mean baring one's "soul" and indiscriminately revealing the intimacies of one's private life. But it does mean a willingness to share more of what one really is as a total person. Listen to how top-level managers of one of our largest corporations did it. Our setting is a meeting of several top managers, migrant workers who are employed by them in an agricultural division of the corporation, and consultants. A manager is talking:

> "I want to tell you first, speaking for all of us in the company, how truly sorry we are because it took us much too long to come here and sit down with you and learn for ourselves what you are up against.... The one word, as I see it, with which to try to explain our long neglect is ignorance. We just didn't know what was happening here, and I'll have to admit, we took the easy way. Sitting here among you today and feeling good because I know we have finally made a beginning in resolving our mutual problems, I have, nevertheless, to deal with the question I know must be on all your minds, 'Why didn't we get together as we are today eight years ago when we first took over the groves?' And the answer, I believe I've made clear by now, is that we took the easy way out, didn't ourselves investigate your working—and living—conditions in these groves..."[6]

And another top manager, speaking later on in the same project, demonstrated another way of being multidimensional. He had opened up a sharing session by telling how he was born and brought up on a small country town in Texas:

> "Prejudice was part of our country life in my hometown. I don't think I ever gave it much thought until just recently. Now I am beginning to see that the problem is not somebody else's problem. It is mine and it is all of ours. I hope you folks can help me with it. I hope we can all help one another."[7]

What one shares is always voluntary and subject to personal feelings and inhibitions. However, the important thing is that leaders embrace the concept that it is important for the people of their group to see them outside of their obvious role.

[6]Sara Harris and Robert F. Allen, *The Quiet Revolution* (New York: Rawson, Wade Publishers, 1978), p. 60.
[7]From taped interview conducted in preparation for *The Quiet Revolution* (September 1970).

Commitment That Shows

It is important for the leader to be committed to the changes that are sought by the group and, further, to be thoroughly committed to the cultural approach.

Leadership requires a belief in what you're doing. If you don't believe in it yourself, it will be very, very hard to help anyone else to do it.

Leaders need to share their excitement, enthusiasm, and ideas with others. Effective leaders don't stand back, afraid to influence others, but are able to share their visions while holding themselves open to the influence of others and the modification or extension of those visions. This is in contrast to the usual situation, in which leaders don't even consider that others below them in the hierarchy would have a vision of what could be.

But even more important is that this commitment show. It is not enough to be enthusiastic if it is hidden under a barrel. It will be more contagious if it is allowed to touch others. Leaders need to be aware of the importance of modeling behavior. What they do is infinitely more powerful than what they say or write down in memos.

Commitment needs to be shown in action. Allocation of money and personnel to a project shows that commitment. Allocation of a manager's time to the early planning meetings shows that commitment. Changes in a manager's behavior, in line with the new norms that have been decided upon, demonstrate the commitment, giving it visibility.

Commitment shows in small things and large. The leader needs to examine his or her actions to see if they are demonstrating the verbal commitment or whether they are, in fact, counteracting it.

A Word About Women Leaders

In Chinese philosophy, the active, masculine force of the universe is *yang*, whereas its opposite, the passive, feminine force, is designated *yin*. In our country most of our leadership roles have been too much on the *yang* axis. It is unfortunate that as women gravitate more and more into leadership roles, they are asked to behave like men rather than just be themselves. In many business circles today a great deal of energy is spent on teaching women executives how to get rid of their warmth and gentleness and their greater willingness to share feelings. This generates two errors: The first is to assign such qualities only to the female. This is a cultural determination rather than a biological one. The second is to give up the opportunity to inject more very much needed qualities into the leadership role—whether the leader be male or female. The openness, compassion, and concern for people that are typically associated with femininity are qualities that are needed by all leaders.

But You Don't Have to Be Perfect

As we said earlier, it is not necessary for managers to have achieved their own goals (health goals, for example, in a culture-based health program) in order to be effective. It is only necessary to be personally involved in the process, show commitment, and get started toward change. It is not necessary for OD practitioners who are working with an organization to improve its sense of community to be paragons of human warmth—but it is necessary to show that they are trying to achieve it on a personal level as well as for the organization.

No one really expects perfection—and often we don't really like it when we see it in others—but it does help a change program to get off the ground for the leaders to be openly and visibly modeling the new norms, no matter how imperfectly.

HOW A CHANGE AGENT
GETS THINGS STARTED

It takes two to tango—but only one to start the music. Any one person can help to get cultural change started. The role can begin with the broaching of an idea to just one other person or by getting a new group together or by going to an already formed group and turning on "the music." He or she can present some ideas about change that will be the beginning of new norms for that group, making it a positive mini-culture within the negative outer culture.

The way that that one person functions will vary according to his or her position in the organization or community. It's easier if you're president of the company or the mayor of the town, but you don't have to be in the top position to initiate change. Other people, at other levels in the hierarchy, can also get things started.

The head of a company or of a community might make use of the system described in the latter part of chapter 2. Other people within the company or community may first want to develop their own support networks and approach the management later.

There are a lot of different ways for programs to be introduced into a company. Sometimes they are part of a total organization development effort, but other times they are initiated by one individual who sees the possibilities of change.

A Starter Set of Tools

In our cultural change programs, we have found some tools to be particularly helpful. Especially designed for leaders in the Organizational Leadership Development Series mentioned earlier, these are individual and group self-instructional programs in key areas of organizational concern.

Another valuable tool is the norm indicator on leadership, shown in appendix C. "As I See It..," the basic norm indicator for organizations (appendix B), which was covered extensively in chapter 4 can be used by leaders to get others interested in exploring the possibilities of using a cultural change approach. Shortened versions of this indicator are helpful in getting people acquainted with the cultural viewpoint.

Also valuable as an opener is the support barometer (see chapter 4), which, as we saw, comes in many variations, depending on the problem needing attention.

How Fred Did It

Fred was manager of the sales division of a large manufacturing company. He had been an outstanding engineer and as a result had been promoted to a managerial position. Most of the managers he had worked under had come from the old school and he, at first, tried to imitate their approaches. However, he was soon dissatisfied with the competitiveness, politics, and lack of togetherness he felt throughout the company.

Then Fred learned about the concept of the manager as culture change agent and decided to try this new approach. "What do you think of how we're doing around here?" he asked some of his fellow managers. "Are there some improvements possible? Are there some things we could do better?"

Fred met with a variety of responses, ranging from deeply rooted negatives to full support:

- complete apathy ("Forget it, you can't change human nature.")
- blame placing and putdowns ("Someone up there won't allow it, and you and I know who that is!")
- a feeling of futility ("We've already tried it, and it doesn't work.")
- skepticism ("Sounds like you're wearing your rose-colored glasses to think that anything might change around here.")
- a beginning interest ("Yes, let's talk about it.")
- complete concordance ("Yes, I'd like to work with you on it.")

Fred listened carefully and made use of many of the ideas that were suggested. Most important, he built upon the positive responses. He used the four-phased change process as a framework and the principles of cultural change as a constant guide.

Fred's first step toward change was to focus on understanding cultures. Fred responded to the negatives with, "Why do we feel helpless around here? Not because we can't, but because it's the norm around here for people to say and think that nothing will happen. If we accept that norm without changing it, we're defeated from the start. Instead, even a few of us can get together and say, 'Let's have a new norm in our group.'"

He then invited a group of his most interested colleagues to dinner one evening, and they discussed some norms that were getting in the way of organizational change. Together they planned some small but immediate steps:

> "One thing we could do is to get a few others together and discuss some possibilities."
> "Let's put it on the board agenda to spend a few minutes brainstorming about what we'd really like to see happening around here."
> "Let's use a support barometer and see what the picture is here."

One doesn't have to shoot for the moon the first day of the project. The small immediate steps that bring at least some immediate results are important beginnings: They start a forward movement, getting us off dead center. They bring us a feeling of hope that change can happen because it already has, because we see it in small but definite ways. People begin to explore new ideas, to look forward to what can be, to examine their dissatisfactions in a new way.

Fred found that one of the most helpful ways to get off dead center was to suggest to people that they stop using their energy to find fault. "Let's not spend time pointing our finger at others. It doesn't matter so much who's to blame. The problem is, what do we do next? Let's focus our energy on that."

The change agent's role is to be constantly alert, aware that people can only too easily slip back into the old way of looking to place blame for problems. The leader needs to be constantly checking for this trend and reminding the group when they get off the track. "Aren't we falling into the old trap of blaming the victim here?" Fred found that such statements had to be repeated many times—and most important, he found that he himself needed to reflect the new norms in his own daily behavior.

Fred and his associates set up a plan for evaluating how they were doing and met regularly to review progress and consider new possibilities and alternatives.

TOMORROW'S LEADERS

Maccoby pointed out a sad truth about today's corporate world in *The Gamesman* when he said, "Corporate work stimulates and rewards qualities of the head and not of the heart. Those [of 250 most admired individuals within the best companies of the United States] who were active and interested in their work moved ahead in the modern corporation, while those who were the most compassionate were more likely to suffer severe emotional conflicts."[8]

We believe that the leaders of tomorrow will have heart and furthermore that they will be "leading" in a supportive environ-

[8]Maccoby, *The Gamesman*, p. 43.

ment, where compassion is rewarded and qualities of the heart are stimulated, accepted, and encouraged. We believe that the most effective corporate leader will use both head and heart and that the two aspects will not be in conflict—for both intelligence and compassion will be in the service of human freedom.

III
HOW TO TREAT
SOME PERSISTENT
PROBLEMS

chapter eight
Organizational Ethics: A Cultural View

The need for developing supportive cultural environments is self-evident when we consider the ethics of much of the business world today. Here we can see the discouraging results of a pervasive lack of "community" and the ineffectiveness of some traditional approaches to change.

This became very clear to me a few years ago when we were involved in negotiations with one of America's largest and most respected corporations. A vice-president of the corporation was speaking of the ethical position of his company. "Ethics can have nothing to do with business," he said, somewhat wistfully. "A corporation is in business to make money, and that is all that matters."

In the subsequent negotiations he backed up his statement with deeds, breaking a number of earlier agreements while saying he was sure we would understand. He couldn't risk his neck for promises, no matter how he felt about them.

If this were an isolated case, one might enjoy berating the individual executive. Unfortunately, his organization's behavior is the rule rather than the exception. In a University of Pennsylvania survey, people in ten countries were asked whether they thought executives in a drug company, faced with the knowledge that their recently developed medication would be dangerous and could kill as well as cure, would take the drug off the market. All the respondents believed the decision would be to continue marketing the drug, although 97 percent believed the decision was irresponsible. "We reached the shocking conclusion," says J. Scott Armstrong, director of the study, "that managers see their responsibility to the company and to its prime goal, which is making money."[1]

In company after company, and in community after community, similar processes are at work. People are behaving in ways that they are ashamed of and are explaining their behavior in terms of "natural" tendencies and "the way things are."

As individuals we are almost all affected. How many of us have, at one time or another, become part of a new group or organization with the idea that we would work to change some of the things that seemed to be wrong with what was happening there, only to find ourselves five or ten years later fully involved in the same behavior that we had once rejected?

CAUGHT IN THE GAP

If the behaviors that we were involved in were ones that pleased us, then perhaps the situation would not be so bad. But that, unfortunately, is rarely the case. The great gaps that exist between what we say we want and what we do in fact achieve are mute testimony to the negative influence of the cultures in which we live.

Even those of us who are most successful at playing the game are not all that pleased with what is occurring. Picture, for example, the young woman employee of a large public service company that we recently studied. She wanted to get to the top, but she realized that, particularly as a woman, in order to get there she was going to have to get and keep a competitive edge on her colleagues. She knew some things that would be helpful to some of the people with whom she worked, but she didn't feel that she could share these with them lest her competitive edge be reduced.

As she spoke to an interviewer about this situation, she lamented her predicament, but felt that there was little she could do about it under the circumstances. "This is a competitive world," she said, "and all of the others are doing the same thing. When I

[1]"The Corporate Mindset," *Human Behavior*, December 1978, p. 50.

get my promotion, I will be able to let them in on my secrets, but by then I will have moved beyond that level and will no longer be in competition with them. I'll have other people to compete with then."

"Isn't that difficult?" the interviewer asked. "Some of these people are probably close to you."

"They are close, and it is difficult," she said, "but you have to do some difficult things if you want to get to the top."

SOME ATTEMPTS TO CHANGE

There is genuine concern about these social patterns in some circles. Observers of the social scene are speculating about "the new narcissism" (Peter Marin), "the Me Decade" (Tom Wolfe), "self-absorption rather than social change," (Edwin Schur), "the politics of self-interest" (Richard Sennett), and "the culture of narcissism" (Christopher Lasch).

Here and there steps are being taken. A few corporations are giving ethics courses to their employees, and last year the country's first Conference on Businesses That Teach Ethics was held, involving twenty-four representatives from companies and universities across the nation. The host was a major chemical company that had for the past seven years offered a three-day ethics course to its top and upper management. Product safety and environmental concerns seem to be key concerns, spurred on by governmental, media, and public pressure.

This activity can be seen as a hopeful beginning. But unless it is implemented in a way that strengthens cultural supports for change, it too will be an opportunity lost. Companies that are interested in ethics as a way to forestall government regulations are not likely to hold onto the positive changes once the public eye is no longer on them. Energy-saving and ecological measures that eat into bottom-line figures will be short-lived, unless the norms of the underlying organizational culture are changed.

Too often, ethical concerns lead only to lip service. One typical company has a Charter Statement of Ethical Goals prominently displayed by all senior executives. However, other than an occasional meeting when the statement may be referred to, very little is done to assure its implementation. As one executive said, "It is for display purposes, not for everyday use."

One wonders about the fate of a similar move in government circles: Recently a law was passed requiring all federal offices with twenty or more employees to display the code of ethics for government service.

Most organizational efforts to show ethical improvement that we have observed have come about as a result of efforts to appease pressures from outside sources. A vice-president of social policy said recently, "My job is to make sure that the issues are dealt with here before they are discussed in the halls of Congress." A teacher of business students said that teaching ethics in college is sometimes "little more than how to get around OSHA."[2]

Corporations that are caught giving bribes or illegal political contributions provide loud *mea culpas* and usually end up firing a few people, sometimes after providing them with large retirement payments to make up for the trouble they are being caused. The basic system is allowed to remain pretty much unscathed.

THE BAD SEED?

It happens not only in our corporations but in our colleges and universities, hospitals, unions, churches, and even in our often sacrosanct agencies such as the FBI, CIA, and the office of the president. The narcissistic syndrome of "me-firstism" prevails in much of our Western culture.

How come? Is it "a bad seed"—an inborn trait of selfishness and greed that is part of our human heredity? Is it some territorial imperative that we are working out as a result of our animal ancestry, a biological equivalent of the survival mechanism of other animals?

Such explanations have been offered, but there is little scientific evidence to support them. They do temporarily "excuse" us, but at the same time they suggest almost nothing in the way of solutions and deny the possibilities for change that exist within us. Accepting such pseudo-biological explanations means giving up

[2]Susan Trausch, "Business Rethinks Practices with New Emphasis on Ethics," *Boston Globe*, April 27, 1981. Reprinted courtesy of *The Boston Globe*.

hope for much of the human race and miring ourselves even more deeply in the backwaters of cynicism and despair.

There are alternative explanations, however, stemming from current knowledge of cultures and their impact on the people associated with them.

THE TRAGEDY OF THE IK

The Ik, a group of nomadic hunters in a mountainous region of East Africa, experienced even more stringent ethical difficulties than we have encountered in our society, with even more disastrous results. Their experience can help us understand more fully what is happening to us.

In the early 1960s Colin Turnbull, a field anthropologist from the American Museum of Natural History, was looking for a suitable group to study in this area. Though he knew little about the Ik, his earlier experiences in Africa had demonstrated that hunting groups were unusually kind, generous, honest, compassionate, hospitable, and charitable. He visualized himself being welcomed by a warm and friendly people.[3]

Upon his arrival in East Africa, Turnbull found, to his horror, that he had been wrong on all counts. The Ik were not only unkind, but heartless; not only stingy, but maliciously grasping; not only dishonest, but cunningly deceitful. They were selfish and ruthlessly cruel beyond the imagination. They pushed their children out of the home at three years of age to fend for themselves— and then stole food from them. They stole from the elderly, the weak, the blind. The strongest men grabbed the limited food supplies for themselves. Old people were frequently left alone in their huts to die.

For two incredible years Turnbull lived among these people, watching as in their struggle for survival they lost all values of family, friendship, and community. Had they always been so bad, he wondered? From the old people he found that they had not. Once they had been a responsible and friendly people with strong family ties extending over an entire village of people. Although there were no written records, there was ample evidence in their

[3]Colin Turnbull, *The Mountain People* (New York: Simon and Schuster, 1972).

language that until recently they had held high values of morality, including loving attitudes toward their fellow human beings. In less than three generations the Ik had lost all vestiges of their former goodness.

Turnbull found that there were reasons close at hand for the Ik's deterioration. Severe food shortages growing out of a ten-year drought had been complicated by new government policies restricting hunting opportunities. Under pressure that threatened their individual survival, the Ik had responded by giving up their basic humanity. Beyond these immediate reasons there were deeper ones that hold lessons for us all: The Ik were unable to cope cooperatively with change.

THE IK IN OUR MIDST

This tragic transformation of the Ik people is, while more extreme than most that we experience, unfortunately not an exception in today's world. Many of us and the groups we are part of seem to be in the process of becoming similarly transformed. Though our bellies are full, we have become, as the poet T. S. Eliot said, the "hollow men" of a modern, affluent, immoral "wasteland." With very little effort of the imagination, we can discover the Ik demonstrating survival tactics in the office, the classroom, the committee and board room. From the smallest work group on the assembly line to the largest international gathering, we are faced with evidence of an Ik-like inability to operate with compassion, generosity, and loving concern. Time and time again we see the values of friendship and community give way to a ruthless "lifeboat" mentality of selfish individualism. This is especially apparent in our business and governmental organizations where, as Christopher Lasch puts it, "the dense interpersonal environment of modern bureaucracy, in which work assumes an abstract quality almost divorced from performance, by its very nature elicits and often rewards a narcissistic response."[4]

Like the Ik's culture, our organizational cultures can change drastically. One company we had the good fortune to work with

[4]Christopher Lasch, *The Culture of Narcissism*. (New York: Norton, 1979), p. 96.

some twenty years ago was shockingly changed when we visited it recently. People who had once cared deeply for one another and demonstrated high levels of creativity and innovation had become bureaucraticized and uncaring, both in their work and in their interrelationships. The company had grown in size, but had shrunk in quality. Its earlier dynamism had become only a memory in the minds of the few who had originally created it.

Interviews were conducted with both the old and the new employees. The explanations given were mostly in terms of who had been to blame for the perceived failure and how the people who were now with the company were "a totally different lot than the group we used to have." In point of fact, there was not much difference between the old and the new employees, but the environment itself had changed rather drastically. No matter how fondly they looked upon the past, the old employees manifested almost identical attitudes and behavior patterns to those of their newer compatriots. And these attitudes were quite different from those they had demonstrated twenty years earlier. "We were naive then," one old-timer said. "We didn't know how selfish and self-centered most people really are. It's a dog-eat-dog world," he summarized.

What had happened to cause such a dramatic change in the people's behavior? Certainly something more than individual choice was at work here.

There were reasons for these changes, as there were reasons for the changes in the Ik group. In this case, it was not because of food shortages affecting the physical environment and ultimately the culture. But there could be no doubt that a new cultural environment had been created in the company. In its quest for success it had lost both its success and its humanity.

PRIMITIVE CHANGE STRATEGIES

Sometimes companies like these do attempt to bring about organization-wide change—making a real moral commitment to higher ethics and better human relations. Unfortunately, these well-intentioned efforts often fare as badly as their poorly intentioned counterparts. There are a number of reasons why this is so, having to do with the primitiveness of the change strategies employed.

These change strategies usually begin with a focus on the individual transgressor. In our society we tend to blame the individual for almost everything, usually with very unfortunate results.

Blaming the Victim

The head of a large public utilities company called us a few years ago asking for advice. He had recently been called upon to fire one of his management employees because he had found that he had been "fudging" the production statistics. This had been a great surprise to him, but the real shock had come when he found that the other managers at the same level as the manager who had been fired were very upset by the president's decision. He couldn't understand how this could be. Had they all lost their sense of morality and ethics to such an extent that they weren't outraged by one of their members acting in this way? Our investigation of the situation showed that the manager who had been caught and fired had in fact been following the cultural norm for his group and that if he had not fudged his production statistics, he probably would have been fired a good deal earlier, since all of the other managers were lying about theirs.

Blaming the victim is a well-established approach to keeping things the way they are in our society. Thus the ghetto dweller is blamed for the litter in his community; the sales executive for his "excesses," which can usually be defined more narrowly as "getting caught"; the West Point cadet for his cheating within a cheating environment; the policeman for taking graft within a culture that has made this a way of life; the competitive young executive for refusing to work cooperatively with his fellow executives. It would help us a great deal more if we would devote a much more significant percentage of our energies to finding out what in the situation had encouraged the behavior that concerned us.

By focusing exclusively on the individual, we think we free ourselves and our organizations from complicity in what is happening around us. The recent firing of a few top executives of a number of our major corporations for corrupt dealings with government agencies gave some people a feeling that morality had perhaps at last returned to the business environment. But certain troubling questions remained if we had cared to look at them. Why had these people offered bribes to foreign governments in the first place? Had it been their own individual immorality? Or had it been the custom and norms of the organizations that they belonged to and of the larger business community and governmental structures within which these organizations did business? How long, one might ask, would the vice-president of sales of Aircraft Corporation A hold that position if the vice-president of sales of Aircraft Corporation B managed to bribe his or her way into most of the billion-dollar sales opportunities in this highly competitive situation? The same appears to be true for the various investigative committees that appear from time to time in our political landscape. How well did the Kefauver Committee do on putting a stop to organized crime in America? How well did the Knapp Commission do on ending police corruption in New York City? How well did the Watergate investigations do on eradicating corruption in our political life?

This is not to say at all that there may not be some value in identifying individual transgressions. It is to say, however, that if we focus exclusively on individual transgressions, very little of lasting value is likely to be accomplished.

Supermarket Theft

A study of employee theft in American supermarket companies revealed the way a culture creates its victims and then blames them. Young people were being employed by the company to serve as cashiers who manned the checkout stands. A typical orientation pattern was seen to exist. It had little to do with the orientation program provided by the company, but it was much more effective. It worked like this.

The new employee, a young man named Ken, joined the company and was quickly welcomed and made to feel at home by the other employees with whom he worked. He was invited to join them in the bowling league and to engage in other social functions. He was learning to feel quite comfortable and was learning his job well. After a few weeks he was assigned his own responsibility at a checkout stand.

It was then that one of the other employees asked Ken if he would be willing to "discount" some of her friends when they came in to shop the next afternoon. He wasn't sure what the term *discounting* meant, but when he found out, he was quite shocked. *Discounting* meant "not charging them for the meat or something," his fellow employee explained. When she saw his concern, she said, "Everybody does it around here. There is nothing wrong with it. We will be doing it for your friends, too." He reluctantly agreed, after considering the alternatives, which included losing his new friends and perhaps even his job if enough of his new "friends" became his enemies. After a few weeks he became a little more comfortable with the practice and even helped to invent some new approaches to it.

Some would suggest that Ken should have had the courage of his own convictions in such a situation, and some people do. However, that is quite a lot to ask of a young person who likes his new job and his new friends and could well lose both as a result of his nonparticipation. Ken could be blamed for his dishonesty, as could most of Ken's fellow employees, but Ken and his colleagues were much more the victims than the perpetrators, and blaming them does little to help us focus on the underlying problem.

One of our great philosophers once suggested that a society is in jeopardy when a person has to be a martyr or a fool to do the right thing. Such is the case in many of our organizations.

Simplistic Solutions Fail

In addition to our undue focus on individual solutions and blame placing as approaches to change, there is also a tendency in our society to rely on overly simplistic solutions to complex cultural problems. This is not only true of the company president whose initial actions to promote teamwork were described above, but also of more sophisticated social scientific approaches as well. One of the most common of these approaches calls for undue reliance on economic and technological variables.

From this vantage point all that is necessary to bring about positive change is to rearrange the economics and technological factors affecting what is occuring. Thus if we remove the economic need for stealing, stealing will no longer be necessary, and therefore will not occur. Unfortunately, this theoretical position is unsupported by the data that are available. If it were true, we might expect that a multimillionaire executive would have little motivation for dishonesty once his or her economic needs were taken care of and that people in our upper-income brackets would be less destructively competitive than people of lower-income levels.

Neither happens to be the case, and it is clear to most of us that cultural patterns of motivation, once formed, tend to maintain themselves even after the original economic and technological conditions are modified. This does not mean that economic and technological factors are unimportant, but rather that they must be dealt with in a broader cultural context if they are to produce and maintain positive change effectively.

BUT IT *CAN* HAPPEN HERE

If changing the precipitating economic and technological conditions is not sufficient and if focusing on the individual problem is unlikely to succeed, then what can be done to bring about lasting change in cultures such as ours? Are people doomed to repeat the mistakes of the past, or are there ways people can come together to change the environments that are changing them?

Fortunately, our experience with a variety of cultural change programs suggests that there really is something people can do to change their environments. It is possible for us not only to understand what is happening to us, but to bring about the changes we want. We *can* come together and develop the sense of community and build the supportive environments that are needed to make the kind of world we would like to have for ourselves and for posterity. Using the systematic cultural change process suggested earlier (see chapter 2), people can change the negative ethical patterns of their organization's unconscious and establish norms that support higher ethical standards.

To start to discover the norms that influence ethics in your organization, you might try the following questionnaire with your associates:

WHAT KIND OF ETHICS DO WE SUPPORT?*

Please check on the right the box that you think best describes the level of support in our organization.

How are we doing in our organization in providing an environment that consistently encourages people

	VERY POORLY	POORLY	SOME BUT NOT ENOUGH	WELL	VERY WELL
1. to treat each other with dignity and respect?	☐	☐	☐	☐	☐
2. to be honest and open in their dealings with one another?	☐	☐	☐	☐	☐
3. to be fair in their business dealings, even if it is to the organization's disadvantage?	☐	☐	☐	☐	☐
4. to refuse to take advantage of people, even when it might be helpful to the organization?	☐	☐	☐	☐	☐
5. to behave ethically in their relationships with one another?	☐	☐	☐	☐	☐
6. to behave unethically in their relationships with one another?	☐	☐	☐	☐	☐
7. to do whatever is necessary to beat each other out for jobs, promotions?	☐	☐	☐	☐	☐
8. to use unfair competitive practices when necessary to win?	☐	☐	☐	☐	☐
9. to so emphasize winning that it is more important than the human values involved?	☐	☐	☐	☐	☐
10. to act in terms of their own ethical concerns?	☐	☐	☐	☐	☐
11. to overlook their own ethical concerns when this would be useful to the organization?	☐	☐	☐	☐	☐

	VERY POORLY	POORLY	SOME BUT NOT ENOUGH	WELL	VERY WELL
12. to build deep and meaningful relationships with one another?	☐	☐	☐	☐	☐
13. to maintain relatively superficial relationships with one another?	☐	☐	☐	☐	☐
14. to discriminate against certain groups or individuals when this is thought to be beneficial to the company?	☐	☐	☐	☐	☐
15. to look upon some people as more significant and more worthy of consideration than others?	☐	☐	☐	☐	☐
16. to look upon some people as less significant and less worthy of consideration than others?	☐	☐	☐	☐	☐
17. at the lower rungs of the organizational ladder to be treated with less dignity and respect than people at the upper levels?	☐	☐	☐	☐	☐
18. to see the bottom line (profit, productivity, sales, etc.) as being more important than ethics or relationships between people?	☐	☐	☐	☐	☐
19. to state organizational goals almost exclusively in terms of quantitative as opposed to human and qualitative results?	☐	☐	☐	☐	☐
20. to participate in destructive competition between people and organizational units within the same company?	☐	☐	☐	☐	☐
21. to feel that human values have little to do with everyday business activities?	☐	☐	☐	☐	☐
22. to tell one person one thing and another something quite different?	☐	☐	☐	☐	☐
23. to be dishonest in their relationships with one another?	☐	☐	☐	☐	☐
24. to be constructively honest in their relationships with one another?	☐	☐	☐	☐	☐

117

	VERY POORLY	POORLY	SOME BUT NOT ENOUGH	WELL	VERY WELL
25. not to talk with people they may have problems with as opposed to constructively discussing the problems?	☐	☐	☐	☐	☐
26. to feel that their first responsibility needs to be to themselves and their own well-being?	☐	☐	☐	☐	☐
27. to hide their feelings from one another?	☐	☐	☐	☐	☐
28. to stand behind their promises no matter how difficult this might seem?	☐	☐	☐	☐	☐
29. to protect their own neck first no matter what effect it has upon others?	☐	☐	☐	☐	☐
30. to be open and honest in their dealings with one another?	☐	☐	☐	☐	☐
31. to be considerate of the feelings and concerns of those they work with or supervise?	☐	☐	☐	☐	☐
32. to be cooperative?	☐	☐	☐	☐	☐
33. to treat all people with respect and dignity?	☐	☐	☐	☐	☐

Summary questions

To behave honestly and caringly in their relationships with one another?	☐	☐	☐	☐	☐
Not to behave honestly and caringly in their relationships with one another?	☐	☐	☐	☐	☐

For an additional instrument that can be used to help people become more aware of the level of cultural support for poor ethics, see appendix D.

chapter nine

The Absenteeism Culture: Becoming Attendance Oriented

When an organization tries to handle its problem of absenteeism without dealing with its "unconscious," it usually ends up in failure. One large corporation we know of gives us the picture: A company-wide fight on absenteesim was launched; new attendance-control systems were installed; corporate executives let people know, "We mean business this time"; bulletin boards and company newsletters talked of little else. The employees, after some initial resistance, seemed to go along, masking their underlying feeling that "this too shall pass." After three months absenteeism had decreased 50 percent, and several thousand dollars had been saved. Even the early doubters had to admit that the "results" had indeed been secured. But that was the last of the good news. The next three-month period saw a little slippage, as did each succeeding three-month period. Although a hurriedly administered booster shot moved things up temporarily, two years later attendance had dropped—in fact, it had dropped *below* the original preprogram level.

A CULTURAL MATTER

We live in an absenteeism culture. Taking a day off and calling in sick is supported and encouraged by our society. Many people's attitude is, "The time is coming to us."

119

Employers are also guilty of supporting absenteeism as a cultural phenomenon. They *expect* people to take sick days when they aren't sick and accept it as one of the costs of doing business. Absenteeism is so routine that employers budget around it, make overtime allowances for it, and hire more workers than they need to take up the slack it causes.

What does this absenteeism culture cost? Estimates of its cost to American business exceed $100 million a year. But this figure does not account for losses in productivity resulting from workers covering for one another, missed deadlines, missed orders and meetings, blown opportunities, and other substantial costs. As is well known, large numbers of people say that they are sick when in point of fact they are not. This is such a widespread practice that most workers would think of it as more of a fringe benefit than as dishonesty. This practice, which costs our American economy billions of dollars a year, is actually figured into the cost of doing business in most companies.

Many employers do try to do something about it. The business community spends millions of dollars every day on programs designed to hold absenteeism down to acceptable limits and reduce its rate of growth. When measured by old yardsticks, some of these programs look successful. Human resources managers take pride in impressive before-and-after statistics on the reduction in absences and person-hours saved, as well as other indicators of better attendance. They also point out with pride new policies and procedures, communications materials, and other elements of successful campaigns to reduce absenteeism.

Why, then, is it frequently necessary to start all over when those same indexes show absenteeism on the rise again six months, a year, or eighteen months later?

The answer has less to do with how well managers use these programs than it does with the environment upon which the programs are imposed. Absenteeism is a cultural problem. To beat it, a cultural solution is needed.

FERRETING OUT ATTENDANCE NORMS

Recently we were doing a study of absenteeism in one of our major American corporations. Employees interviewed as part of this research suggested that the company itself often encouraged such dishonesty by the way it dealt with the problem, that is, penalizing individuals who were honest enough to give the actual reasons for their absence. As the employees saw it, the company was encouraging employee dishonesty and deepening problems of absenteeism.

To be sure, not all employees were involved in such practices. Some managed to maintain a distance from this widespread cultural phenomenon. It was interesting to note, however, that employees who were hired within a department with a low absenteeism record were more likely to keep their own absenteeism time down than those hired into a department with a higher absenteeism record. This type of absenteeism is clearly a matter of attendance norms.

Considerable disparity was evident in another company in the absenteeism rates between similar work crews. Investigation showed that absenteeism was directly traceable to the group norms established by the leadership, the environment, and group expectations. Each group had similar accident and illness records. It was the norms that dictated, almost predictably, whether people showed up for work.

Absenteeism has its own subtle but complex norms. These norms are supported by the culture outside the workplace and are shaped by the work culture itself. They are often symptoms of larger organizational problems. Norms in the following areas influence people either to work or to stay home, thus helping create the absenteeism culture:

LEADERSHIP COMMITMENT.

Managerial commitment to attendance goals and its views toward absenteeism do have an important impact on attendance. In one manufacturing company, a manager who demonstrated little commitment to sound attendance practices had one of the highest absenteeism rates in his organization.

LEADERSHIP MODELING.

What leaders say about absenteeism is often less important than the way their behavior is viewed by other organization members. A vice-president in one company often worked at home but never explained her regimen to those under her. Her department was high in absenteeism. When she looked into the situation, she was surprised to find that her employees felt she had been goofing off and not working a full schedule.

RECOGNITION AND COMPENSATION SYSTEMS.

Employees frequently remark that there is no advantage in reporting for work every day, because no one seems to care. A supervisor reduced absenteeism by 40 percent when letters were written for personnel files for each six-month period of perfect attendance, with copies sent to conscientious employees.

ORGANIZATION POLICIES AND PROCEDURES.

Regulations can sometimes cause more problems than they prevent. Sometimes they actually get in the way of good attendance practices. Being five minutes late, even for a good reason, is often looked on less favorably than taking a sick day.

SUPERVISORY INTERPRETATION AND IMPLEMENTATION OF POLICIES.

The personal link between employees and supervisors can be used in shaping a program. One supervisor tried a positive approach to absenteeism by starting a telephone follow-up to absent employees, expressing concern for the cause of their absence and offering help to them and their families.

RECRUITMENT AND SELECTION.

Employers ask for information about attendance in reference requests too infrequently. One candidate for a managerial position had an impressive work record, but he also liked to keep Mondays free, a fact that went unnoticed because references were not checked.

EMPLOYEE ORIENTATION AND TRAINING.

Attendance norms are established the first day on the job. In a supermarket with low absenteeism, the importance of good attendance and exposure to high-attendance employees was stressed during orientations for new cashiers.

PERFORMANCE APPRAISAL.

Performance appraisal procedures can boost good attendance practices. If attendance rates make a difference in raises and appraisals of performance, and if employees are aware that this imformation is part of ongoing performance appraisals, attendance patterns are affected. A change in management's emphasis on attendance as a factor in performance appraisal caused an uproar in one department, where the employees thought it was an entirely new policy.

HEALTH FACTORS.

The connection between health and absenteeism is often overlooked or narrowly defined, with little attention being paid to alcoholism, drug abuse, and other stress-related factors. A supervisor checking on the absenteeism of one employee found it was caused by a drinking problem and helped that person enter a program for problem drinkers.

JOB SATISFACTION.

Boredom on the job is frequently ignored; little attention is paid to making the job more interesting or explaining its importance within the organizational framework. A group of shipping employees with a high absenteeism record improved attendance when the supervisors paid attention to job enrichment by explaining the importance of the job in the company's marketing and distribution program.

RELATIONSHIP OF ATTENDANCE
TO SPECIFIC EVENTS.

Vacations, holidays, meetings, training sessions, and other events influence the rate of absenteeism. One plant in a rural area checked with its employees and decided to close down its whole operation the first day of hunting season. Positive results in both morale and attendance were noted.

The norms of absenteeism cut across many areas, as can be seen in the typical comments shown in the following list of negative comments. These expressions describe "the way things are around here" and represent several of the more common negative norms found in our absenteeism culture.

What They Are Saying . . .
(Comments Indicative of Negative Norms)

"You can get around it. Just don't take Monday or Friday off, and it won't show up in their records."

"There's no reward for coming in, no punishment if we're out, so what the hell?"

"We've got personal time coming to us. If they don't want us to take the day, they shouldn't have offered it to us."

"It's a fringe benefit. Everybody does it."

"I'm going to get paid anyway."

"There's no time clock. It means the company isn't all that concerned."

"They're doing all right. They can afford my days off."

"I get in more hot water for being fifteen minutes late than I do for taking a sick day."

"Don't worry about the dispensary if you're out more than two days. They just sign you back in."

"There's always somebody to cover for you around here. Nobody's going to miss me."

The persistence of these negative norms encourages absenteeism and necessitates managerial planning to allow for absent workers. If 10 percent of the workers are absent, their absence is an imposition on the others, affects work scheduling, and adds other costs that push the price of absenteeism far beyond one day's salary.

Corporations often try to *manage* negative norms. In the process, they accept a continuing cycle, consisting of an absenteeism reduction program, followed by a return to the old way of doing things, followed by another absenteeism reduction program. A breakdown of the negative norms shows why these periodic campaigns have so little long-term effect.

In many corporations, executives manage the absenteeism problem by making it a function of personnel, training and development, or other human resources managers. Executives may write memos, suggest meetings, and stimulate commitment in other ways; however, the prevailing norms can mislead them about their level of responsibility. One negative norm states that "absenteeism is a personnel (training and development or human resources) matter, so I'll put Jack on it." Jack accepts the duty, but he does not share the responsibility for solving the problem. Thus absenteeism remains just another cost of doing business. It becomes a fringe benefit taken advantage of by employees and is accepted as a way of life by both them and top management.

CULTURAL CHANGE REQUIRES SYSTEMATIC EFFORT

Although norms are necessary to the human condition, they can be changed, especially in light of the malleability of an organization's culture. To change an absenteeism culture, a systematic effort must be based on changing norms in the following areas:

INVOLVEMENT OF EMPLOYEES
AT ALL LEVELS.
From the chief executive officer to the supervisor to the new employee, involvement is crucial. Each has some kind of direct impact on an organization and contributes to the modeling, rewarding, or supporting of attendance norms. Involvement means more than assigning tasks. Since everyone is affected by change, everyone must participate in shaping change, from goal setting at the start to final implementation.

RESULTS ORIENTATION.
Baseline and periodic measurements of attendance, productivity related to attendance, and attendance norms produce data that can be clearly communicated to the entire organization.

SOUND DATA.
Accurate preprogram analysis and record keeping assure getting the kind of sound data a program should be based on. This information enables managers to make higher quality decisions in setting attendance goals.

A POSITIVE FOCUS.
Punishment intensifies resistance. Giving managers the tools to recognize and reward employees who maintain good attendance records stimulates personal and cultural change.

A SYSTEMATIC APPROACH.

Change must be concerned with the factors that influence attendance norms so that managers can improve their skills and build a more effective organization.

FOLLOW-THROUGH.

Since the change process is an ongoing, participatory commitment, management has the opportunity to review, renew, and sustain attendance goals periodically.

CREATING AN ATTENDANCE CULTURE

No one would argue that every employee can or should be convinced to come to work every day; most of us do fall ill from time to time. However, an attendance-oriented culture with *an attendance way of life* can be created. Change requires a complete corporate commitment to encourage attendance rather than manage absenteeism. This is a significant shift, because an absenteeism culture not only costs millions of dollars a year but also stifles the development of human resources, dulls an organization's competitive edge, and sabotages profits.

The cultural change process outlined here has reversed prevailing norms in dozens of companies. One dramatic achievement took place in an agricultural project where, in a three-year effort, migrant workers changed their culture drastically. Attendance records were boosted by 40 percent, replacing probably the worst and longest record of absenteeism in the country with one as low as that for any other part of the company, including the one for white-collar workers.

There is probably no more graphic illustration of an absenteeism culture than the one existing in parts of Scandinavia, where absenteeism runs 25 percent or more. Research indicates that the reasons for not coming to work there are more often related to the culture than to illness or other readily identifiable factors. Employee perceptions of their work affect why people work or do not. If absenteeism in these countries is to be reduced, culture-based programs hold more hope for progress than the more usual measure of merely combatting absence.

Some companies have tied absenteeism reduction programs in with a health program. By focusing on preventive health care and creating a healthy culture built on positive health practices, a significant decrease in absenteeism is predictable. People who are taught how to lengthen and improve the quality of their lives are less apt to be sick. They are also more likely to take pride in their work, their accomplishments, and the culture that makes them possible.

Other less dramatic but equally satisfying achievements (in terms of both productivity increase and lift in employee morale) have been experienced in warehouses, offices, supermarkets, and plants using the Normative Systems approach:

- An agricultural project reduced absences from a two-day-per-week average per worker to a one-half-day average.
- A distribution center warehouse improved attendance by 25 percent.
- A pharmaceuticals company reduced absenteeism by 31 percent over a one-year period.

A Case Study

The Awl-Time Corporation provides its thousands of employees with excellent benefits, top salaries, and attractive job situations. Survey after survey of employee attitudes has confirmed that view, and more than five thousand people apply for a job with this company every month. Absenteeism at Awl-Time is therefore all the more enigmatic as a problem. Why do people who struggle to get a job in this corporation and who believe it treats them well stay away from work so often?

Like many corporations, Awl-Time measured and managed absenteeism without questioning cultural influences on it. Month after month, a recently appointed vice-president of personnel watched the high rate of absenteeism with alarm. He was concerned with the corporation's productivity and recognized attendance as being an important way to keep a competitive advantage. He calculated that absenteeism represented a bottom-line loss totaling more than $1 million a year in hourly time alone.

He recognized that an absenteeism culture had become well entrenched. The vice-president's findings sparked formation of a

Corporate Attendance Task Force (CAT) a couple of years ago to find out why absenteeism was climbing by more than 1 percent per year.

The CAT team discovered that absenteeism was not recognized as being a problem by either salaried or hourly employees. Confronted with the facts, many employees tended to reject the data. The work ethic, they said, was strong in their company. But surveys and recommendations by consultants confirmed the scope of the problem.

Change started at the top. The corporation made a full commitment to the CAT team, and a systematic cultural change was begun with a thorough analysis of all the areas that influence attendance. Sophisticated testing devices helped pinpoint the norms operating in each area.

Goals were set, and division vice-presidents committed themselves to new attendance standards. Implementation teams from the personnel and training unit worked with managers and supervisors in all divisions to outline the change process. Line management people became trainers and carried the change process throughout the organization. Policies were rewritten, the rewards and recognition system was modified, and the results were communicated to all employees. In departments where absenteeism had led to overstaffing, employees were given an option to be retrained and transferred to other departments.

In the most recent Awl-Time report on absenteeism, the results of the program indicate an impressive gain in attendance. The absentee rate for the previous year had been 5.9 percent, with an estimated cost to the company of close to $2 million; the latest absentee figures indicate a drop of more than 1.2 percent, saving the company approximately $500,000 in one year alone.

The change process continues. Managers and supervisors at Awl-Time are working at changing the absenteeism culture on the spot. They immediately and constructively confront negative attendance whenever it occurs, clearly state the attendance behavior they expect, model that behavior, and encourage those who maintain good attendance records. The following comments are in sharp contrast to those indicative of negative norms:

What They Are Saying . . .
(Comments Indicative of Positive Norms)

"Look, if I'm not in, it screws up the whole schedule."

"I get hassled when somebody doesn't show up. I don't want to do that to somebody else."

"The last time I was out, the supervisor called every day and dropped my check off at the house on payday. He calls everybody who's out, even for a day."

"We've got targets to meet, and that takes teamwork."

"I was out for a day last week, and this morning a VP tells me he's glad I'm back on the job."

"The less you're out, the more money you make."

"They've got a lot of benefits around here, including a free checkup whenever you're out sick."

The building of an attendance culture can benefit from other organizational improvement efforts and contributes to them as well. The involvement of Awl-Time's line managers established a successful approach to dealing with problems by offering them training in organizational leadership and development. Such organizational leadership modules include a series of workshops, practical exercises, and printed materials that stress high involvement, on-the-job results, and an ongoing feedback system. Awl-Time's line managers were helped to

- gain an understanding of the problem
- develop a shared commitment to its solution
- develop counseling and confrontation skills
- plan and implement a systematic program

After one year of use, this module for improving attendance has netted impressive results. These results are not produced by the modules, the consultants, or the training unit. Rather, they are cultural changes, improvements produced by line managers—from the shipping department all the way up to the executive committee.

chapter ten
Treating Corporations as Cultures: Five Cases

What actually happens in a corporation when it takes a cultural approach to change? This chapter reviews the highlights of five corporate programs that successfully made use of the methods and principles we have been discussing. The case logs below represent a cross-section of business organizations and include the following:

- Two supermarket companies (King's Supermarkets Inc. and Purity Supreme) that desired to reduce their waste, or "shrink," factor from an excessive 3 percent of total sales
- A multinational soft drink and food company (Coca-Cola Foods Division) that desired to overturn the migrant-worker pattern of its agricultural operation
- A West Coast sales district servicing the fast food restaurant business that desired to reverse a two-year history of no profit
- A newly opened unionized distribution center that desired to meet the critical challenges created by a wildcat strike and a poor production rate
- A pharmaceutical manufacturing company (Hoffmann–LaRoche) with a history of remarkable growth and earnings that desired to develop a more open and participative supervisory style as well as a stronger profit center orientation

In the initial analysis of each of these organizational settings, we found a common thread of prevailing skepticism that "when you really get down to it, you really can't change things." Comments made by members of each of these organizations during the introductory interviews with them demonstrate the various forms this negative feeling can take.

- Case 1 *Two Supermarket Companies*
"Shrink has always been 3 percent of sales in this business. We just have to live with it." "Our employees couldn't care less about shrink."
- Case 2 *An Agricultural Company*
"What? Not charge them for their ice? And give them field toilets? Where is this program ever going to stop?"
- Case 3 *A Fast Food Sales District*
"These fast food operators are not like the restaurant owners of the old days." "The company expects us to be unprofitable in LA." "You just can't sell coffee anymore the way you used to."
- Case 4 *A Distribution Center*
"Screw the company. They'll never care about us, and we'll never care about them." "It's us against them. Either we win or they will." "Look, I became executive vice-president by coming up through the school of hard knocks. It's all I know. And these warehouse-people, they're animals. It's all they know."
- Case 5 *A Chemical Division of a Pharmaceutical Company*
"You'll never change the eighth [executive] floor." "Look, we've got training programs up the kazoo—and all that has never changed a thing."

With this kind of widespread feeling about the lack of potential for organizational change, it is no wonder that most efforts to change organizations have tended to be halfhearted, piecemeal, simplistic, unsustained, and usually focused on blame placing and scapegoating rather than on developing all-win solutions.

In spite of this lack of faith in the possibility for change, people still feel the need for some sort of "magic" formula to solve chronic problems in their organizations. The Normative Systems approach of viewing organizations in cultural terms often helps meet this need. A successful intervention by a change agent downplays the mystical "magic" of his or her solution and leaves the members of the organization realizing that they had the potential within themselves to effect the desired change.

APPLYING
THE CULTURAL CHANGE MODEL

Step 1. Analyzing the Existing Culture:
Establishing a Norm Gap

As we have seen, the first step in the Normative Systems process involves analyzing the existing culture and setting specific objectives for the change effort. In a total OD program, this stage in the process includes discussions with workers, leaders, and key opinion makers; the administering of survey instruments; observation at operational meetings; direct participation in workplace activities; informal off-the-job interactions; taped interviews; and analysis of existing performance and bottom-line results.

Organizational leadership and work teams are key to the identification of existing and desired norms in critical influence areas. The desired culture is expressed in the form of a set of specific objectives that can be measured regularly and that are accepted throughout the organization as realistic and worthwhile indications of the kind of change that people desire in their organization's functioning. The process of identifying the norms of the existing and desired cultures establishes a "norm gap." The juxtaposition of the performance objectives with the norm gap forms a clear statement of the goals for organizational change and provides the baseline and target measurements for the change program. Progress toward closing this gap is regularly measured.

The five corporations of our case logs all found the following eight influence areas critical to this ongoing evaluation process.

1. *Leadership Modeling Behavior.* An organization's culture is tremendously influenced by the behavior of the people with the most authority and power. Behavior throughout the organization is affected not by what top management pays lip service to, nor even by what it actually does, but rather by what leaders are perceived as doing, by what appears to get their attention and their priority.

2. *Work Team Culture.* Every work team has a culture. Every worker is part of a work team that has a specific subculture of its own. This subculture is often formed, reinforced, and even modi-

fied at informal meetings of the work team at which, for the most part, supervision is not present. At these informal gatherings, the work team examines, develops, and reinforces its particular work team culture. Getting supervision involved and helping the work team develop a positive and contributing culture are the most important activities for achieving sustained change in the workplace.

3. *Information and Communication Systems.* Our definition of *culture* is "a set of expected and supported behaviors." Most of the communication of this support and expectation is through words, both written and oral. The type of information and the way it is communicated in a culture have a powerful impact on the behavior that is expected. Areas where data is sparse or poorly communicated tend to receive much less attention than areas where information flow is accurate and consistent.

4. *Performance and Reward Systems.* Cultures and the normative behavior within cultures are influenced by what is "appraised" and ultimately rewarded and/or recognized. Too often, reward systems actually interfere with the development of positive cultures and sustained achievement.

5. *Organizational Policies, Structures, Budgets, and Procedures.* Organizational policies and procedures convey clear messages from the power structure as to the organization's cultural priorities. Unfortunately, many of these policies, structures, budgets, and procedures support prior cultures and patterns of expected behavior that are no longer valued by either employees or management.

6. *Training and Orientation.* While most individuals are in fact open to cultural influence at "teachable moments" during their first day(s) in a new work environment, most people find that what is taught in the training or orientation is ignored, put down, or even counteracted in the actual work team culture back on the job.

7. *First-Line Supervisory Performance.* In our experience, most companies contain two distinct cultures engaged in win-lose game playing, which all too often deteriorates into both sides losing. We have found that first-line supervisors are usually expected to bridge these two cultures but are given neither the tools, the climate, nor the support necessary to accomplish this difficult assignment.

8. *Results Orientation.* Because there is so much skepticism about being able to change organizational cultures, we have found that it is absolutely necessary to state specific, measurable objectives that everyone agrees will, upon accomplishment, constitute satisfactory achievement and cultural change. Once the objectives are set, progress toward achieving them will need to be monitored. Data showing this progress needs to be gathered at regular intervals, and then feedback provided to the people. This will help support and give confidence to those who initially became committed and continue to work toward change. It will also serve to convince skeptics and provide data on which to base the program. Most organizations have many skeptics—people who will not try to change until they begin to experience it happening around them.

The following chart illustrates by means of our five case histories, the specific norms identified in both the existing and the desired cultures, as well as the objectives set during this first phase of the project.

Case	Sample Negative Norms	Some Specific Objectives
The Supermarket Companies	Employees accept a 3% shrink, and no one is confronted about it. Department and store managers are not informed regularly of the amount of their shrink.	Shrink will be reduced to 2% in 9 months and to less than 1.5% in 18 months. Within 1 year every store employee will be involved in an effective shrink-control program. Within 1 year every department and store manager will be setting specific goals and receiving monthly feedback. These managers will be accordingly rewarded for effective shrink control.

Case	Sample Negative Norms	Some Specific Objectives
The Agricultural Company	Absenteeism averages 2 days a week, and turnover is around 400%. Productivity and income levels are low. Employees' standard of living is substandard when measured in such terms as housing, child development, social services, and cultural enrichment. The company expresses insufficient concern for the welfare of its employees.	Absenteeism will be reduced to 1 day a week. Productivity and income will at least double within 18 months. No employee is to live in substandard housing. Accredited and/or licensed community facilities in child development, social services, and library services will be opened within 2 years.
The Fast Food Sales District	Sensing lack of headquarters' interest in this district, its employees assume that the loss situation is tolerated and expected.	The following profit objectives will be met: Break-even within 6 months and 10% profit within 12 months.
The Distribution Center	Employees feel that the interaction mode between company and union will always be us versus them.	Productivity will increase from 117 pieces an hour to 150 pieces an hour. Within 1 year, surveys will indicate employee support of and identification with the company. At the next union negotiation, the company president and labor negotiator will experience less hostility and a greater willingness to strive for win-win solutions.

Case	Sample Negative Norms	Some Specific Objectives
The Chemical Division of a Pharmaceutical Company	Communication is one-way; down from the "eighth" floor. We've been such a successful company that cost-effectiveness, morale problems, and improved communication are no one's concern.	The basic managerial style will shift from being somewhat paternalistic and inaccessible to being significantly participatory and accessible. Productivity (cost/kilo) will increase by a given percentage. Within 1 year a division-wide cost-effectiveness program will be operational, and a results-orientation toward reward for performance will be part of the culture.

Step 2. Experiencing the Desired Culture: Systems Introduction and Involvement

The second step in changing an organizational culture is to give all members of the organization opportunities

- to participate in determining their preferred organizational culture
- to share their frustrations about the negative "norms" existing in their culture
- to experience "neutral ground" where they can examine existing behavior, set individual and group goals, experiment with new behavior, and receive feedback from co-workers
- to experience the feelings they will have about the new culture
- to make a commitment to the objectives they and their organization will be striving toward

In our work with hundreds of organizations, we find that people at all levels of the organization need actually to experience the positive culture being sought. Merely writing or talking about it will fall on skeptical ears. People need an occasion, a happening, to shake them loose from their old traditions. This event, which we call a Normative Systems workshop, serves as a benchmark from which they can begin to measure change.

In the workshop a shared vision of the new, desired organizational culture is experienced, and the workshop itself becomes an ideal, "a peak cultural experience" that is not easily forgotten. Usually this experience consists of a three-day workshop for management, a two-day workshop for supervisors, and a one-and-a-half day workshop for all other employees. The pattern that the workshop design typically follows is shown in the following chart:

Normative Systems Workshop Design and Objectives

Activity	Objective
Introduction	Demonstrate organization's commitment to this change process.
	Convince participants that other organizations have achieved bottom-line results through cultural change programs.
Understanding Your Company as a Culture	Shift attention to corporate or organizational problem solving and away from such single-issue or oversimplified approaches as placing blame on one group and changing individual or group behavior without changing the corporate culture.
	Give people insight into the reasons why it is so frustrating to try to change individual and group behavior without first effecting changes in the organizational culture.
Indentifying the Existing and the Desired Norms You Would Like in Your Organization's Culture	Provide edited tapes, written materials, and other media to enable participants to identify and discuss existing negative norms and desired positive norms honestly.
Changing Your Organization's Culture	Provide specific strategies for changing the organizational culture.
	Inform any participants of change activity to date.

Activity	Objective
	Provide experiences in human-factor aspects of the desired culture through sharing and feedback.
	Demonstrate the tenacity of old culture through exercises on win-lose.
Sustaining the Change	Obtain commitment to shared goals.
	Develop specific on-the-job activities and measurement techniques to support the change effort.
	Determine immediate actions that can initially demonstrate this commitment to change.
	Introduce and schedule ongoing work team meetings to serve as cultural renewal sessions.

Step 3. Modifying the Existing Culture: Systems Installation

Following the involvement workshops, the implementation process begins. This third step in the change program is particularly critical. In fact, absence of a systematic installation phase in many organizational efforts has blocked success of the change effort. Too many companies' efforts, unfortunately, never proceed beyond the development of a report on the problem or, at best, the initiation of a series of training sessions, meetings, and activities. What really changes organizational cultures are the critical norm influence areas. Accordingly, step 3 in the Normative Systems process focuses specifically on these influences.

The effort proceeds simultaneously along three lines, all working to modify the critical change factors within the culture. First, leadership is engaged in an improvement program focusing on leadership's role in each influence area. A "training" module in each area provides an assessment of the area's existing leadership behavior, an identification of its desired leadership behavior, a content input for improving behavior, and simulated on-the-job demonstrations of the desired behavior. "Instructors" or "coaches" for this leadership program are line managers and supervisors who have demonstrated on-the-job success in the change area.

Secondly, the participants in the step 2 workshops are organized into action-study task forces. The goal of these task forces, which include all levels of employees, is to study the areas within the corporate environment that influence the organizational improvement process. Action-study groups delineate problem areas and recommend implementation strategies in each of the critical cultural influence areas. These action-study groups are ongoing to ensure the continual application of these change influences.

Thirdly, all organizational work teams begin to meet regularly to improve their own on-the-job culture. Specific training is given to each work team leader to develop his or her group's culture. Regular work team meetings are held within a structured format that provides regular opportunities for the group to receive feedback on its performance; to focus on issues, suggestions, and areas of concern; and to work on problems confronting the group.

Since the norm-gap analysis performed in step 1 typically indicates a need for improvement in some areas more than in others, the change effort in each organization is tailored to its special needs. The following sampling from two of our case logs illustrates these different intervention areas, describing specific actions taken to modify the expected behavior.

The Agricultural Company
Organizational policies, structures, budgets, and procedures. A carefully selected corporate vice-president was transferred from the home office to provide on-site support for the change program. A multimillion-dollar budget was set aside for the effort.

LEADERSHIP MODELING BEHAVIOR.
Executives at corporate headquarters spent great amounts of on-site time planning and evaluating program performance. These executives and the on-site vice-president attended every function that was considered critical to the success of the program. Additionally, the on-site vice-president devoted twelve or fourteen hours of each day to the project in its initial stages and often worked equally long hours on the weekends. Most of this activity involved direct contact with the migrant population.

TRAINING AND ORIENTATION.

The corporate officers and all supervisors attended a series of high-impact training workshops. At the kickoff workshop, the corporate president announced that any executive or manager who would not support this effort to upgrade the working and living conditions of his migrant or seasonal workers should resign immediately or face termination. Ongoing workshops in human relations and leadership skills were provided for management, workers, and project staff.

WORK TEAM CULTURE.

Every effort was made to maximize worker involvement in the planning and decision-making phases of this project. The focus of the project was shifted away from a "welfare" culture to a self-help culture by the establishment of community boards responsible for budgets and programs, worker management committees, worker involvement with the architect-planners, and a project staff drawn from the worker population.

RESULTS ORIENTATION
AND ACCOMPLISHMENT.

Nevertheless, it was only after a new community replaced old company housing, health facilities and child development centers were actually opened, and workers began to experience year-round work and fringe benefits that the great majority of workers and management began to believe that the company was serious in its change efforts.

*The Chemical Division
of a Pharmaceutical Company*

ORGANIZATIONAL POLICIES, STRUCTURES,
BUDGETS, AND PROCEDURES.

Because the company had recently reorganized the more than 800-person production area into a profit center by combining it with chemical marketing, the program was initiated with a new vice-president and director in charge. A very competent, internal OD staff (one full-time and two part-time employees) was made available and worked in close partnership with the outside consultants. Within twelve months of project initiation, a reorganization of the chemical production area was accomplished that resulted in a leaner, more flexible, and less bureaucratic organization. Complete organization restructuring has occurred that utilizes the maximum managerial expertise available.

INFORMATION AND COMMUNICATION.
For the first time in the division's history, relevant work-related information was provided at all levels. Twelve action-study groups including exempt and nonexempt employees began working in all of the change-strategy areas. Work team performance charts providing regular feedback on task accomplishment and work team culture charts providing regular feedback on team building were generated by the employees in norm areas. Systems installation should be completed within six months. Information flow and feedback with such supporting departments as maintenance, management information services, marketing, and quality control have improved.

WORK TEAM CULTURE.
Employees began to meet bi-weekly with their work teams and supervisors. These interactions supported and renewed the positive experience of the Normative Systems workshop.

FIRST-LINE
SUPERVISORY PERFORMANCE.
Extensive on-the-job supervisory training was provided including videotapes of supervisors conducting meetings and performance reviews. Middle management became directly involved and responsible for upgrading first-line supervisory performance.

Step 4. Sustaining the Desired Culture:
Ongoing Evaluation and Renewal

As results are achieved, the focus shifts to sustaining the emerging positive culture. Just as regular evaluation is critical throughout the installation phase in order to measure progress toward objectives clearly, ongoing evaluation is necessary to ensure sustained results and to disclose the need for retooling and renewal of the change effort in one or more influence areas. To be successful in the long term, this process must become a permanent aspect of the organization.

Measurement of the results is conducted along both normative and performance dimensions. Survey instruments are used to measure modified perception of behavior in each influence area, and charts are used to monitor performance objectives including bottom-line results.

The results achieved and sustained in our case histories are outlined below.

THE SUPERMARKET COMPANIES.

Shrink dropped from 3 percent to approximately 1 percent in one company and to 1.8 percent in the other company in which this program was introduced. These results have been sustained over the years.

THE AGRICULTURAL COMPANY.

Annual wages and productivity increased by a factor of two. Turnover dropped within a year and a half to less than 100 percent. Absenteeism became as low as that in any other part of the company, including white-collar areas. Community facilities in health, child development, library services, and tutoring became models for the entire state and began to attract noncompany funding.

THE FAST FOOD SALES DISTRICT.

The district broke even within two months and continued to maintain a satisfactory profit level.

THE DISTRIBUTION CENTER.

Productivity increased from 120 pieces selected per hour to 146.7 pieces per hour. Turnover was reduced dramatically, and absenteeism and damage loss decreased by 25 percent and 50 percent respectively. The company reported that negotiations with the union were no longer being conducted in a hostile and mutually belligerent climate. The union has begun to ask that other companies utilize the same type of program in their distribution centers.

THE CHEMICAL DIVISION.

Twelve months into the program, there were many indications that the organization's culture had changed. Communications and both middle-management and employee involvement increased markedly. Problem-solving styles, morale, and cost effectiveness improved. Productivity levels were maintained despite a 20 percent personnel transfer and a drastic reduction of overtime. The division that had once been considered less prestigious in the corporation became a leader in effective and innovative organizational procedures.

WHY EFFORTS TO CHANGE THE ORGANIZATIONAL CULTURE OFTEN FAIL

In our experience with corporate cultural change programs, we have had a number of failures, particularly during some of our earlier applications. Studying failures can lead to a better understanding of why cultural change efforts within organizations can fail to achieve their objectives. We have identified eight common pitfalls that not only result in a waste of time and money but, even worse, build expectations that, unmet, only escalate the cynicism, apathy, and frustration that characterize many organizational cultures.

1. *Lip-service commitment from the chief executive officer.* In a hierachical structure such as a business, the visible modeling behavior and gut-level commitment and involvement of the president and most of his executive staff are essential. Lack of understanding or visible support from the top has often frustrated change efforts.

2. *Adherence to traditional win-lose attitudes.* The change effort will fail unless it reflects a win-win approach to change. Focusing on scapegoating or recriminating individuals or groups for past mistakes severely impedes a cultural change program. In our experience, we find that people welcome the cessation of blame placing.

3. *Inadequate involvement of all levels of employees.* Employees will not believe in the effort unless they have an opportunity to help plan it, provide feedback, experience it (not just hear about it), and develop a sense of ownership in the change process.

4. *Insufficient attention to middle management*. These employees often see themselves as guardians of the status quo (culture) and often see change programs as "the latest thing that the president has brought back from the last conference he attended." They then go into a pendulum mode: shift with the new program for three months or so and assume that everything will and should go back to normal again.

5. *Insufficient support of first-line supervision*. The culture gap or clash is usually most severe between employees (usually of the younger generation) and the older first-line supervisors who have been promoted not for their supervisory skills but for loyalty and hard work.

6. *Inappropriate pace to the change effort*. The error is to move either too slowly to build momentum and confidence or too fast and thus interfere with daily operations, which turns it into a taxing and ultimately wearing effort.

7. *Inappropriate level of expectation*. Given that people basically do not believe they can change organizations, the need for leadership to truly believe that the organization can change is essential. On the other hand, changing a human culture requires a systematic effort over time. Thus, while we have invariably found an immediate positive response to our workshops, expectation of bottom-line results in less than six to eighteen months is unrealistic.

8. *Failure to internalize the change process*. The external professional plays a crucial role in the change program in terms of providing an objective analysis of the existing culture, training the members in the concept and methodology of change, refining and modeling the application of the change strategies, and evaluating early results. However, a critical element of the change program is the assumption of the change agent role by both organizational leadership and all members of the culture. If the change process does not become internalized and a permanent part of the organizational function, the program's accomplishments will not be maintained.

NOT FOR EXPERTS ONLY

Transactional analysis, with its "parent/child/adult" and "games" framework, is an attempt to make the principles and practice of psychotherapeutic intervention more readily understandable and available to the layperson with a minimum of training. Similarly, the cultural change approach we suggest tends to make the principles and practice of organizational intervention and development understandable and available to non–behavioral scientists and nonexperts.

In most of our successful interventions, the reaction has been, "This is a kind of common sense approach. It helps us apply what we already know in a systematic way and in a way that most of my line people can buy into."

chapter eleven
Quality of Work Life: A Cure for Hospitals

Kay Hopkins had some ideas that might have been helpful to the hospital. But unfortunately, they never got applied.

She liked nursing and cared a lot about her patients, but somehow it was the little things that were getting in her way. It wasn't the hard work that bothered her. She was used to that. It wasn't the pay, which, although low, was no less than her peers'. Kay's concern was the lack of communication and the impersonality of the hospital. She had a feeling that with the exception of a few close associates, no one knew her name. People seldom asked for her ideas or listened when she presented them. There were directives that didn't make sense and were never explained except with a shrug and a "Don't ask me, they just do it that way around here."

Finally, there came one bad Friday in her tenth year of nursing. That day she wrestled with Dietary to get an extra salad for a patient; she had a battle with Laundry to get some sheets; and it took her three hours to get Housekeeping to help her clean up a mess of broken dishes when a patient tipped over his bed tray. She had just worked a double shift and realized that in a few weeks she'd be going from day to night duty again. She wondered where to turn with her complaints, but all around her were others with problems no less difficult than hers. Exhausted and frustrated, and thinking of her three-year-old child at the day care center, she quit. It was another case of hospital work-life "burnout."

ANALYZING THE NEED

Three hundred thousand other nurses could tell stories similar to Kay's. Of the 1.4 million registered nurses in this country, 25 percent no longer practice. Hospitals currently report about 100,000 nursing vacancies. Eighty-eight percent of our hospitals have been unable to fill available positions, and fewer people are choosing nursing careers.

While inadequate pay and minimal promotion opportunities are obvious reasons for this severe shortage, just as important, according to nurses who have been interviewed in our projects, are the kinds of problems that Kay ran into.

Recent research corroborates our findings. A three-year project by the Columbia University School of Public Health explored ways to improve practices and procedures for nurses where they work.[1] The project, which involved ten hospitals, found that the factor that most influenced a nurse's ability to carry out her nursing functions was *interpersonal relationships*. Although the nurses had been taught that their practice should be based on knowledge and experience, what actually happened was that they soon found it much easier to simply go along with the traditional ways of doing things. This set up stress-inducing situations and caused frustration and dissatisfaction. There was, understandably, a low level of work satisfaction revealed when the nurses responded to questions about key job characteristics. Freedom from supervision was the job characteristic that received the lowest score. The nurses' responses to other parts of the survey revealed a desire for greater teamwork. They wanted to be "separate but equal" partners as far as professional responsibility was concerned.

It is evident that the quality of work life in many hospitals does not attract or hold the nursing staffs the nation needs. And nurses are not the only hospital employees becoming frustrated. The same appears to be true for other employee groups, ranging from orderlies to administrators and from clerks to staff administrators. No group appears to be exempt. In the growing field of hospital administration (now 180,000 strong), health care administrators struggle with the chronic problems of too little money, too few nurses, constant turnover among low-paid aides, and strict but

[1]"Nursing Practice Project," *American Journal of Nursing*, December 1980, pp. 2127–56.

ever-changing government regulations. These managers have heavy responsibilities and must maintain delicate relations with physicians, trustees, and public officialdom. On top of it all is the reality that many of their decisions mean life or death to someone else. It is important to this group of managers, as well as to nurses, physicians, and patients, that the hospital environment be one of support, teamwork, and good communication.

WHY A QUALITY OF WORK LIFE PROGRAM?

The potential benefits for a hospital from a quality-of-work-life program are many. Some possibilities are

- improved patient care
- reduction in turnover
- reduction in absenteeism
- increased productivity
- higher morale
- better community image
- improved teamwork
- cost savings

Each hospital will need to decide which focus best applies to it. Many of our hospitals will find that all these areas need attention. Many have tried to treat one or more of these problems and have not been satisfied with their efforts. It has been our experience that, when they have failed, it has been primarily because they did not see the cultural basis of the problems.

THE HOSPITAL AS A CULTURE

What does it mean to treat the hospital as a culture? Rather than working piecemeal on rectifying particular negative factors, we focus on building positive ones, that is, molding the hospital environment into one in which an open, flexible, participatory, voluntary, shared change process is a way of work life. This is not to say that gripes and complaints are to be ignored. Certainly the notorious low pay of many hospital employees is more than a mere gripe—it is an important problem to be confronted.[2] But raising salary levels is not the total answer, nor even the most important part of the answer.

To change the quality of any work environment, one must first make an adequate analysis of the problem and then carry out a systematic program based on the crucial areas that are revealed. It is not enough just to find out what the problems are; one must also look at the total situation in terms of *what the culture supports*. In this case the culture is the total organizational environment of the hospital, including staff, employees, nurses, and patients. Does the hospital environment accept and support extra-long working hours? Is it the norm of the hospital culture to expect people to hide their emotions and feelings from one another? Is it a cultural norm in the institution to ignore areas of stress that create tension among staff members? Is it the norm to leave it up to individuals to find their own solutions?

SOME TYPICAL HOSPITAL NORMS

Norms can be either negative or positive—that is, norms that contribute to the low quality of the environment or ones that make it an attractive and satisfying place to work. They can be clustered in areas such as norms of performance and excellence, norms of teamwork, norms of communication, norms of patient relations, norms of training and development, norms of leadership and supervision, norms of problem solving and decision making, norms of innovation and change, norms of organizational pride.

These norms are expressed in a variety of ways:

---

[2]For further background and discussion of the problems of salaries and hospital costs, see Jeff C. Goldsmith, "The Health Care Market: Can Hospitals Survive?" *Harvard Business Review* (September–October 1980); also our own suggestions on cost saving in F. Allen, et al., "Getting into the Wellness Business: Potentials and Pitfalls for Hospitals," The HRI Selected Paper Series. Our basic premise is that hospitals, like major corporations, can effect considerable savings through systematic, culture-based wellness programs.

"Around here, a nurse has to be a supervisor, an administrator, a personnel expert, a coordinator, a statistician, a chart and report maker. I only wanted to be a nurse and take care of patients."

"Around here, you get the idea that the doctors don't trust us nurses. They want us to be flunkies who are seen but not heard."

"Around here an eight-hour shift really means nine hours, because you're expected to stay on to brief the incoming shift."

"Around here nurses are often expected to take on double shifts and to switch from day to night duty every few weeks."

"Sometimes we're expected to take charge of units with which we have no familiarity, just because they need to be able to say someone is there."

"We're overqualified for the tasks they'll let us perform. We have college degrees and are able to perform physical exams, but we can't do it officially—that's only for doctors."

"We're sent out on the floor without knowing what to do."

"Around here, there's no one to turn to to help clarify your ideas and figure out what should be done. You're on your own."

"No one seems to care or notice when you do things right."

"Around here the situation is so full of stress, it is difficult to apply our nursing knowledge."

PATTERNS THAT GET IN THE WAY OF WHAT WE WANT

There are some typical norm patterns that develop in hospitals, often making the hospitals go in directions they really do not want. Institutions that were started as places to further humanitarian ideals can end up cutting them down, making people feel less human and more alienated. Some general patterns that often develop are the following:

DEPENDENCE, OVERPROTECTION,
AND ACQUIESCENCE.
Hospitals tend to treat patients as helpless children, encouraging dependency patterns. The staff overprotects patients, taking away their decision-making powers even in areas in which they are very capable and eroding their sense of self-responsibility. Acquiescence is often the norm for patients and professionals alike, with all tending to go along with the idea that it is only natural for a hospital to make choices for a patient.

NONHELPFULNESS.

Patients are not expected to help one another. Whatever skills or knowledge they have in dealing with others is "put on the shelf" until they are dismissed. It is not the norm for patients to relate to one another, support one another, or take part in building a cooperative environment within the hospital.

DEHUMANIZATION
AND FALSE PROFESSIONALISM.

To many people, being professional means denying feelings, presenting oneself in a role rather than as a whole person. Patients are known as "the cardiac in Room 203." Nurses get caught in a treadmill of nonnursing duties. Administrators feel that to be "professional" is to be tough, decisive, and not give in to feelings.

BUREAUCRATIZATION
AND STRATIFICATION.

Red tape and administrative structures sometimes get top-heavy, keeping people apart and impairing communications between levels. Competition and backbiting between departments develop, getting in the way of a smoothly functioning organization.

APATHY.

Probably the most devastating and difficult pattern of all is the belief that things just can't change, and it's no use trying. This is sometimes expressed by, "That's just the way hospitals are."

THE TOP PROGRAM

To get past these negative patterns and motivate people to help change things and improve the quality of their work life, we have designed a program called TOP (Turning On People), which works with the following six norm areas:

1. *Involvement.* It is the norm for people to be involved in setting their own work objectives and methods in developing organizational structure and problem solving.
2. *Clarity of organization and structure.* It is the norm for people to have a clear understanding of what their job is and how they fit into it.

3. *Feedback and information.* It is the norm for people to get feedback on how well they are doing and information about how their work is contributing to the overall organization.

4. *Orientation and training.* It is the norm for people to receive the orientation and training and get the skills and knowledge they need to do the job well.

5. *Rewards.* It is the norm for people to have their accomplishments rewarded and their positive behavior reinforced.

6. *Supportive culture.* It is the norm for people to get support from the hospital culture and from each other in what they are doing to bring about helpful personal and organizational change.

By working with these variables, a quality-of-work-life program not only can interest people in changing their health practices and work environment but can help them maintain the changes.

APPLYING THE
NORMATIVE SYSTEMS MODEL

PHASE I.

We have already touched upon some aspects of Phase I, namely the analysis of norms in each TOP area, to see how they are affecting the quality of the work environment. Instruments designed for this purpose are available and offer a way to start involving all interested people from the start. During Phase I, this material is collected, and the chosen goals are set up.

PHASE II.

Here the cultural change process and the TOP principles involved are introduced to every layer of the hierarchical structure of the organization, usually starting with the leadership level. Through workshops, people are given a taste of the kind of supportive environment they can build; both personal and group change programs are planned; and managers get help in finding ways to deal with the six TOP change factors.

PHASE III.

The new positive norms are now tried out on a daily basis right in the workplace. The lessons learned in the workshops are translated into practical behavior "on the floor." Task forces and small support groups help people check on their progress in the six TOP areas and share successes.

PHASE IV.

Evaluation of what is happening is a constant, ongoing process. Phase IV provides for both evaluation and renewal efforts. Often yearly evaluations are held, with renewal workshops helping people to renew enthusiasm and modify their plans to fit in with the new daily realities. The instruments used in the analysis can be used again to measure progress and help in planning the points of renewed emphasis.

THROUGH A NURSE'S EYES

To see how a systematic culture-based change program works, we might take a look at it through the actions of some people in the program. Take Nurse Jennings's experience, for example. Her situation was not much different from that of Nurse Hopkins, of our earlier example—until she became involved in a TOP program in her hospital. She volunteered to join the planning committee when invitations were first issued to all members of the staff. The invitation announced the program and asked people interested in playing an initial leadership role to come to an exploratory meeting. She completed the norm indicator and later helped tabulate the results of a number of these, joining in on the discussion of goals that followed.

A few weeks later Nurse Jennings took part in a half-day introductory workshop. There was a film describing the cultural approach to change and explaining the important principles involved. With eighteen other people—doctors, orderlies, clerks, nurses—she took part in human relations exercises and small-group activities and came away feeling that for the first time she saw some of her fellow workers as multidimensional people rather than as carriers of certain roles. She drew up some personal goals for herself. One immediate goal was to start taking an extra moment with the patients as she made her rounds, expressing a feeling and encouraging them to express theirs. A second goal was to check for tuition grants to see if she could take a course to further her professional growth. A third goal—a long-range one—was to work with a task force within the hospital exploring the possibilities of developing some wholly new approaches to patient care and positive health promotion.

To help herself implement her change efforts in her day-to-day work, Nurse Jennings joined a small support group and found it a tremendous help. Once a week she met with eight other hospital workers—a cross-section group that included an orderly, two nurse's aides, a doctor, a clerk, and two other nurses. At lunch this group discussed their individual and institutional goals, reviewed progress, and supported each other in carrying out plans.

After three months Nurse Jennings took part in an evaluation workshop, in which the larger group reviewed its progress in improving the work environment. They all took the norm indicator again and renewed their plans for strengthening particular areas. They heard reports from various task forces and formed some new ones.

FROM "BURN-OUT" TO "TURN-ON"

If the nation's hospitals are going to survive their financial woes, if the nursing shortage is going to be alleviated and hospital management problems solved, we are going to have to find ways to make hospitals highly supportive and satisfying environments for the people who work in them. This means more than innovative recruitment methods, more than easier schedules, more than greater salaries and benefits. It primarily means helping the hospital environment become one where interpersonal relationships are enjoyable, where people cooperate, where they trust each other, where good communication is the norm.

There was a time when the pace and atmosphere of the typical hospital was a great deal more warm, personal, and caring than it is now. We have gained in medical technology and efficiency but have lost in terms of human factors. We can't turn the clock back, and we would not want to throw out the miracles of modern medicine that have saved so many lives and rescued so many from illness. But we would like to have those human qualities again—and we are capable of reviving them. When people work together as full human beings, work-life "burn-out" can be replaced by a "turn-on," with benefits for professionals and patients alike.

chapter twelve
Litter Reduction: Treating the "Common Cold" of the Environment

The problem of litter is a touchstone issue, and dealing with it culturally can pave the way for larger and more profound transformations in community life. Litter is a good place for community activation to start, because it is a highly visible social problem that can quickly demonstrate that people, working together in a systematic program, can redesign their cultures.

With this larger framework in mind, one can view with considerable optimism the success of nearly 263 American communities who are taking part in the litter reduction program begun in 1974 as an HRI pilot project and then spreading under the sponsorship of Keep America Beautiful. The program is now called the Clean Community System. Frequent measurements in the three pilot cities have yielded an eight-year record of what a systematic, culture-based approach can achieve—unprecedented litter reduction at low cost.

Prior to the three-cities project, litter programs had been ineffective and expensive. Years of advertising with such slogans as "Don't Be a Litterbug" and "Point Out Pollution" had not done much to stem the tide. Keep America Beautiful (KAB) was dissatisfied, realizing that playing the role of a scolding parent was not working. It decided that a positive, community-based cultural program was worth trying, and pilot projects were set up in Charlotte, North Carolina; Macon, Georgia; and Tampa, Florida.

Significant results were achieved, even in the first year, and continued to get better over the years. The figures tell the tale.

Litter reduction eight months after the project began:

Charlotte, N.C.	40%
Macon, Ga.	25%
Tampa, Fla.	34%

Litter reduction after four years from beginning of project:

Charlotte, N.C.	69.5%
Macon, Ga.	80%
Tampa, Fla.	69%

Litter reduction seven years after the project began:

Charlotte, N.C.	75%
Macon, Ga.	80.3%
Tampa, Fla.	(Not available)

A closer look at our litter culture and the way these cities dealt with it yields some valuable lessons for anyone interested in community activation and change.

OUR LITTER CULTURE

All community problems are cultural, and litter is no exception. Nearly everyone agrees that littering is bad. Advertising slogans scold us and try to put us to shame with phrases like "Don't Be a Litterbug," or "Slobs Litter." Yet we continue to be a littering nation, and for every one person who changes to neater ways, there are dozens who accept the littered environment as "the way things are" and help perpetuate it. Litter seems to be the "common cold" of the environment, the problem everyone censures and no one solves. And it will continue to be such an enigma as long as we turn to individual answers and treat it as a problem of individual rather than cultural change.

The story is generally the same for the towns and cities that have come into the program since the pilot project. KAB figures indicate that people are able not only to make a significant reduction in litter during the enthusiastic first months of a program but to maintain and extend that reduction over the long haul. This means that long-lasting changes in community attitudes and behavior are being achieved.

With these successes in mind, let us look at some of the problems communities run into in trying to change, and see how the litter project handled them.

SOME TYPICAL NEGATIVES

Any community activation effort has to face some tough questions: "How can we get beyond that helpless feeling that things just can't change?" "Once we do manage to change something, how do we maintain it?" "In the age of narcissism, do-it-yourself, hang-onto-individual-rights, people are afraid to sacrifice their narrow self-interest to group needs—how can you get around that?"

These questions point to negative attitudes that pervade most community efforts. People's basic cynicism about their ability to change things, often fostered by the frustration of seeing new ways tried and lost, puts a damper on group efforts. In addition, our tendency to try to place the blame, spending energy on faultfinding rather than on solution finding, and our American proclivity for quick, one-shot solutions further impedes efforts to solve community problems. We find ourselves caught in the cycle of the self-fulfilling prophecy: Because we believe we can't change, we perpetuate the attitudes and behaviors that keep us from changing.

The following basic negative attitudes show up in litter problems as a host of negative cultural norms, all of which support littering behavior:

"Slobs litter, and there are always lots of slobs."
"It's human nature to litter."
"Litter is a part of life."
"People have been littering since the first caveman threw a bone out of his cave."
"As long as there are people, there will be litter."

"We had a Boy Scouts clean-up campaign last year. The town was clean for a few weeks, but now things are back to normal."

"I clean up my yard, but I can't take on the world."

"Nobody really cares, why should I?"

Unfortunately, littering behavior very often is expected and accepted by our groups, and we end up with a network of community support for the very thing we decry. Littering becomes acceptable behavior.

Acceptable behavior? One tends to question this, perhaps thinking of those admonishing commands, such as "Littering is bad!" It *sounds* as though we don't accept littering, but often our actions belie our words. Litter has been a problem for humankind since early times. The prevalence of the talus heap—that mound of trash outside the ancient cave or cliff dwelling that delights archeologists—attests to the early acceptance of littering as a way of life. America has a history of pervasive litter norms. Think of the years of trash on the streets, of auto wrecks cluttering cities and disfiguring the countryside, of papers and rags trapped against fences and buildings for years, of city apartments where people "airmail" garbage onto the streets and empty lots.

The growth of cities and our ecological awareness have only served to highlight a long-standing problem. The crux of the matter is not that people choose to litter, but that they don't give it a second thought. Note that one of the first acts of man on the moon was to litter the moonscape, just "doing what comes naturally."

TEST YOURSELF.

Test the thesis that "littering is a norm." Picture going to two different beaches. One is immaculate, newly raked. The other is full of litter. On which would you be more likely to throw a cigarette stub or candy wrapper? Do you hear yourself saying, "Why not?"

THE SYSTEM LITTERS.

The basic reason people litter is "because other people do." Littering behavior isn't confronted, and likewise nonlittering behavior isn't supported. The quickest way to change individual littering and to maintain the change is to change the culture. To the slogan "Products don't litter, people do," we add, "People in groups or cultures do. It is the system that litters." We tend to litter where we see that others have littered. When we see litter, we usually add to it or fail to confront those who do. If we stopped to question how the litter got there, we might find out it was not thrown by someone, but rather was blown from a neighbor's improperly put-out garbage can. However, the effect is much the same, regardless of the source.

To say that littering is deep within our culture does not mean that everyone litters all the time, but there is some indication that most of us litter when it is socially acceptable—in the baseball park, for example.

If it is the culture that litters, how did the three-cities project make it possible to transform such ingrained normative behavior? What is the difference between that project and less successful efforts?

THE MODEL IN ACTION

The litter reduction project followed the basic Normative Systems model.

Phase I. Finding Out About Litter

The pilot project began with a thorough analysis of the problem, starting with the early history of littering. It was found that through the years many solutions had been tried, with very little lasting effect. Although society has been plagued by more devastating problems, few rank higher than litter in terms of visibility and continuing concern for a solution. Yet litter has continued to accumulate and interfere with the quality of life. The crux of the matter is not that people consciously choose to litter, but that they don't give it a second thought.

The analysis showed that there were a lot of misconceptions about litter, and the program started with careful research to get the facts. The researchers defined litter as "uncontainerized, man-made solid waste," and the outside expert brought in as a consultant listed 150 items (roughly 65 percent paper, 14 percent metal, 7 percent plastic, 5 percent glass, and 10 percent other items, such as clothing, rags, and building materials).

The implications are in the figures. If a program focuses exclusively on banning throw-away bottles and cans, it is probably ignoring about 75 percent of the problem.

Pedestrians and motorists are popularly believed to be the chief sources of litter, but actually there are five other sources that together contribute more: uncovered trucks, loading docks, poor refuse collections, construction and demolition sites, and commercial and household garbage put-outs. This explains why programs to stop motorists and pedestrians from littering have such limited results. People might stop for a while, but then they see trash fallen from an uncovered truck and assume that someone has thrown it, that littering is the norm. So they do it too.

There are essentially four kinds of participants in a littering culture. There are, of course, the actual litterers—people who deliberately or unconsciously litter. Then there are the "gate-keepers," the people in power who make decisions that contribute to littering. They may be judges and police who don't enforce laws or town officials who don't provide sufficient sanitation budgets. Third, there are the "witnesses," who stand silently by without confronting littering behavior, witnesses who up to now haven't had a constructive tool or system for confronting and changing these norms. And finally there are the "victims," who have to live in the littered environment. In a sense, we are all victims. Unfortunately, the worst victims receive the most blame. In HRI's research the most frequent scapegoats found were the poor people from ghetto areas.

A general failure to see the litter problem as culturally determined turned out to be the biggest public misconception. But the pilot project looked upon litter as a people problem and redefined it in cultural terms. The analysis included a study of community problem-solving norms, gathered by the use of depth interviews, surveys, and observations.

By indicting the norm rather than the individual, a more positive approach takes the place of the usual blame placing. If people say "Littering is the expected behavior in this neighborhood," they will get a lot more cooperation in working to change that behavior than if they say "You're slobs," as is suggested by some anti-littering posters.

In the past, many programs have laid heavy emphasis on blaming, especially on blaming the victim. Actually the victim can do very little about the problem if the gatekeepers of the town don't care enough to provide equipment and funds for cleanup and don't enforce the laws; if the major sources of litter—the loading platforms and improper put-outs, the uncovered trucks and the construction sites—are not confronted; and if the witnesses to all this stand silently by.

Analysis showed that though littering was generally condemned, people weren't involved in finding solutions. For example, sanitation workers, who dealt with trash every day, had not been asked to become involved in seeking new and more creative solutions that could make use of their experience.

Out of the analysis a plan was formed, and objectives were set. Both broad and specific objectives were necessary.

Broad objectives:	Reduce litter; develop a model that could be used in a community of any size; substitute a systems approach for simplistic solutions; generate enthusiasm in the local community; develop a program cities across the country could afford.
Specific objectives:	Measure litter regularly and reduce it by 20 percent within twelve months; have a workshop experience for every community member, starting with the "gatekeepers," in which they learn what litter is and what causes it and in which they help plan what must be done to reduce it; develop in each pilot city a community-wide task force to develop and implement a systematic plan for litter reduction.

Phase II. Involving People

Understanding and "shared ownership" were fostered through workshop experiences. A series of workshops was designed to get things started, to introduce the concept of cultural change, and to gain the commitment and involvement of the members of the community. These workshops were offered to everyone, starting with the gatekeepers—government, business, and civic leaders, including public works officials and environmental group leaders. Eventually these workshops were conducted throughout the community.

The workshops consisted of several consciousness-raising components: what litter is, where it comes from, and the dynamics behind it. Through a litter-perception test, people found that litter is "in the eye of the beholder." Slides of various areas were shown on the screen, and people were asked to rate the litter content from 0 to 5. They found that they tended to rate an area higher if the photo was taken on a rainy day or if the neighborhood was rundown.

After a few minutes of this perception test, people got the point. Their perceptions of litter distort the facts. By examining the photographs of litter within the community, they came to see that litter isn't everywhere; it's just in certain locations. It follows, of course, that those are the logical target areas. No wonder generalized cleanup campaigns had done little good!

The workshops played a vital role in helping people to see and understand littering norms and to develop plans for changing them together.

Growing out of the workshops were additional studies of the litter culture, including examination of existing litter technology, sanitation codes, ordinances and enforcement, current programs, community structures, and organization of the central committee. These studies produced recommendations that were eventually refined into the Clean Community System. The plan that resulted provided a blueprint for systematic modification of cultural influences.

Phase III. Changing Things

One of the challenges of community work is the large numbers of people that are usually involved. Interactions and relationships that will foster cooperation and maintain enthusiasm need to be developed. Early results need to be communicated to people to help them see that change is possible and to motivate further action. In addition, community work involves a large number of variables.

Key pressure points have to be selected where crucial areas can be treated without wasting time and energy on peripheral areas.

In implementing change, all seven sources of litter were dealt with, and all four types of litterers were helped to understand and change littering norms. Because norms have to be changed in the situations where people are involved with each other, the community-based program was appropriate. A sign on a highway will not stop littering, but a program back home in the community can change the norm so that even when people get out into the country in their cars, they no longer litter.

A central leadership group acted as a clearinghouse and policy group, with task forces set up to deal with the crucial areas and small support groups to act as reinforcement. This type of administration sees that new norms are installed and that successes are communicated to people, and it offers a flexibility that responds to changing circumstances. (See a suggested chart for community activation in figure 7.)

For a closer look at what Phase III meant in installing a new nonlittering culture, let us transport ourselves to one of the three cities during the early weeks of the project. We see a young man, a lawyer, sitting at a big, circular table. Across from him are a white-haired bank president and a middle-aged sanitation worker. Also at the table are a high school principal, the president of the local women's club, the vice-president of a bottling company, and a behavioral scientist. There is an air of seriousness in the room, but also a sense of achievement, relaxation, and relationship. People from diverse segments of the community have been getting to know one another and learning to work together on common problems and to find solutions in which everyone is a winner. The sanitation worker finds he is listened to as attentively as is the bank president.

This central group keeps in touch with all gatekeepers through task forces. Government officials, businesses, and finally neighborhoods are taking part in a program that is based on community cooperation. Through their workshop experience, they have learned that this means working in groups to get the task done.

Our group around the circular table is working on some key norm influence areas. To them, "focusing on results" has meant

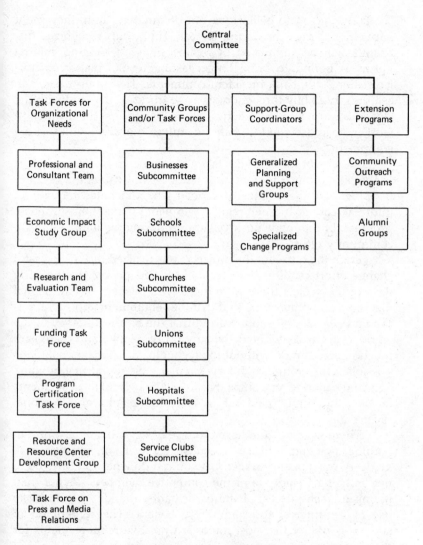

Figure 7. A Community-Activation Organizational Chart. (This basic organizational chart can be modified to meet the needs of a particular problem or community. The type of task forces and support groups will vary accordingly.)

instituting an initial cleanup and removing 80 percent of the litter—most of which had been trapped for years. The group talks about changing the face of the city so that results will be quickly evident.

"Nobody's going to believe we can do anything until they see it happening," says the young lawyer. The group recognizes that change will be stimulated by visible signs. "Changing cultural norms is bound to bring longer-lasting results than restrictive legislation," the bank president comments. The group decides to ask the city to buy three more garbage trucks—"the kind with the closed-in top and automatic feeder," suggests the sanitation worker, "because you lose half the stuff in the street with that old equipment."

A scene of this kind has taken place in each of the three cities in the pilot project. Each established a Clean City central committee much like the one just described which included formal and informal leaders and met regularly to plan interventions, evaluate progress, and provide positive support during the long months of community effort.

From the outset of the project it was realized that a successful change effort requires both technology and people. In the early days of the project there were those who pushed for educational measures and others who said that the "equipment approach" was the panacea. But all soon realized that the best technology in the world won't work without the support of people, and there isn't much people can do without the technology that makes solutions possible. Our group around the circular table found that building and continuing relationships that would be helpful to all segments of the community paid off in statistical results and personal satisfaction.

There were no grandiose promises. Very little, in fact, next to nothing, was said until actual results were in. Then, however, false modesty was not encouraged. "If you can do what you say, you're not bragging," said one of the committee members. Rather than hiding the self-interest of the participants, the idea was to make use of self-interest for community benefit. The recognition of success is one of the most important positive reinforcements for the project.

To deal with the many variables that were at work in the large communities involved in litter reduction, pressure points were selected and targeted for concentrated work. The critical norm influences bearing directly on the litter culture were identified as the following: training and orientation (to clear up misconceptions about litter and to introduce the culture change concept), information/communication (for accurate measurement and effective feedback), involvement of people (by both formal and informal leadership), rewards and recognition (to substitute for blame placing and to reinforce motivation), and results emphasis (careful tracking of achievements and publicizing of results).

By the time of the meeting described earlier, modification of the litter culture through intervention in these critical influence areas was well underway. Integration of field and research components was being carefully coordinated, and attention to this was maintained throughout the project.

Some of the diverse activities that took place under the auspices of the Clean Community System included the following:

MASSIVE EDUCATION CAMPAIGNS,
INCLUDING NORMATIVE-CHANGE WORKSHOPS.

These high-involvement workshops helped clear up misconceptions. In Charlotte, 500 Public Works Department managers, supervisors, enforcement and sanitation employees, and 40 beverage and packing industry representatives attended litter-reduction workshops. In Macon, thousands of people participated in such workshops.

ACCURATE MEASUREMENT OF LITTER
ON A REGULAR BASIS (QUARTERLY)
AND FEEDBACK OF DATA TO THE COMMUNITY.

In each city a baseline for measurement was established, using the latest techniques. For Tampa and Charlotte this was February 1974, for Macon–Bibb County it was April 1974.

DEVELOPMENT OF
UP-TO-DATE SANITATION CODES.

Charlotte particularly stressed vigorous enforcement of all ordinances relating to trash. Tampa placed special emphasis on reduction of litter at the five often-neglected sources. In Macon, the approach was to develop some techniques that could be used by any city that wanted to initiate a Clean City plan.

MEDIA COVERAGE.

Because it was feared that many people might think this was "just another cleanup campaign," actions and results were carefully monitored and publicized. Media coverage was excellent, and soon a belief in the change process became widespread. The media welcomed this opportunity to support litter-reduction efforts through a positive reinforcement strategy. "Look what the people of our city have done," was the keynote, and blame placing and scapegoating were scrupulously avoided. Editorials explaining the project, such as the one in the *Macon News* of May 1974, were helpful. "This is not just another cleanup campaign," it said. "It is an effort to do something about the unhealthy and unsightly problem of litter on a permanent, informed basis by getting at its sources. Macon and Bibb counties are fortunate to be into it on a pilot project level."

AWARDS TO INDIVIDUALS.

Clean City awards were given to people like the grocer in Macon who reorganized his whole day so that incoming grocery shipments wouldn't leave a trail of litter. Public service newspaper ads cited the heroes and heroines of the effort. ("Maude Woods is Pitching in for Tampa.")

PURCHASES OF NEW EQUIPMENT.

In Tampa, twenty new trash receptacles were ordered for the new downtown mall, and eight other styles of containers were ordered to determine the ones most suitable for various locations.

IMPROVEMENTS IN SANITATION SERVICES.

Low-cost-government-housing neighborhoods in Tampa were cleaned up every thirty days by the sanitation department; in Charlotte the street-cleaning program was changed from the "need" basis to a regular twenty-one-area routine covering the entire city.

CLEANUP OF SORE SPOTS.

In Tampa the program was discussed with bar managers on 22nd Street and they agreed to containerize properly. The largest dump in the city was eliminated through a city-industry cooperative effort.

SECURING LEADERSHIP COMMITMENT.

In Macon the city-county government committed a $30,000 budget to the litter-reduction effort and employed an executive coordinator.

Phase IV. Keeping It Going

An important part of any program is the follow-up. Changing cultures is not just a matter of making changes, it also entails maintaining those changes over the long haul. The Normative Systems model recognizes this by providing a final phase that is actually an ongoing one—evaluation (which can start early in the project and be continued throughout), renewal (usually by periodic renewal workshops and reuse of normative instruments to check up on the maintenance of positive norms), and extension (into other cultures, other problems, or other groups within a culture).

When people are acquainted with the complete model early in the community activation effort, they realize that a long-term view is necessary and begin to think beyond quick and temporary solutions.

The three-cities pilot project was able to achieve a cleanup that was long-lasting. The litter-reduction figures far surpassed the original objective of 20 percent in one year, and the percentages kept on climbing, as we saw earlier. Periodic measurements and evaluations of both litter and littering norms were and continue to be an integral part of the program.

Monthly report forms sent to KAB are another tool for evaluating local programs and helping to point out potential problems.

By late 1975 the program was fully implemented by internal resources (no longer dependent on KAB) and was sponsored and run by local leadership. Today there is no need for consultants; the people can do it for themselves.

Though the model and its principles have remained the basis of the Clean Community System approach, there have been a few innovations. One of note is KAB's addition of a certification process and fee for cities wishing to adopt the system. A city applies to KAB, the mayor is briefed and gives the program his or her written endorsement, the director of public works assesses the system and reviews his or her community's litter problem, and the community provides a three-person project team representing government, business/labor, and civic organizations. This team is trained at a KAB workshop and later is responsible for seeing that data are collected and the project is properly coordinated. On-site field counseling is provided by KAB as needed. The KAB communications network circulates news among the certified system communities, and KAB provides recognition to outstanding local efforts through its national awards program.

Occasionally a city is decertified, usually because it allows its program to become just a cleanup campaign rather than a program to change behavior. But over 90 percent of the communities that start the program continue it and experience significant litter reductions. What is more, they find additional benefits in the growth, cooperation, and sharing that give a community a real "sense of community."

chapter thirteen
Health Promotion: Generating Wellness Life-styles

In the field of health, the cultural approach offers a promising alternative. Motivation to change is high, responding to skyrocketing health care costs and greater public realization of the toll taken by life-style-related diseases.

The leader, whether it be the head of a corporation, an OD specialist, the mayor or councilman of a community, or the head of a school or family, has an opportunity to help both the human and the economic picture by introducing a culture-based, participatory system that helps people not only change their personal health practices but also the health norms of their groups.

To illustrate the possibilities of the cultural process in the pursuit of wellness, we will look at it in the context of community activation. The Lifegain Healthy Community System is now being tested in the Pawtucket, Rhode Island, Community Heart Health Program sponsored by the National Institute of Health and is based on the generic Normative Systems model.[1] Other Lifegain projects are underway in corporations, schools, and hospitals.

---

[1]The program is described in *Comprehensive Planning for Community Change: A Case Study of the Pawtucket, Rhode Island, Community Heart Health Program* (New York: American Health Foundation, 1980) and "Community Activation for Risk Reduction," *Proceedings of the Society for Prospective Medicine* (Tucson, Ariz., October 30, 1980). Authors of both articles are Robert F. Allen, Richard A. Carleton, Thomas Lasater, and Charlotte Kraft.

A VISION OF WHAT COULD BE

A community where people support each other in attempts to lose weight? Where young and old jog together—and the community maintains the jogging paths? Where children in elementary school learn to take care of their arteries by eating nutritious foods? A community where no one—almost no one—misuses alcohol or drugs or cigarettes, where people don't drive over the speed limit and just about everyone wears a seat belt?

Too good to be true!

No such town exists—but it could. It could even happen in your community. It is a dream that is becoming more and more possible as people find out what it really takes to reach high-level wellness in a society like ours. And though it will take a great deal of change—for wellness is much more than just being "not ill"—the technology for making such change exists and is ready for use with health promotion on a community level. Perhaps the biggest factor working in favor of the "impossible dream" of a health-oriented community is the availability of a system that has worked for other community problems and for health promotion in organizations and families.

There is a double thrust pushing us in the direction of high-level wellness; the current interest in health and the tremendous need, both in economic and in human terms, to improve our national health practices. Let us look more closely at some of the evidence of this interest and need, before seeing how they can lead to more exciting, innovative community change.

OUR HEALTH BUYING SPREE

Today there is little doubt that America has health on its mind. Ten out of fifteen paperback trade books on the bestseller list concern health. Diet groups, smoke-cessation clubs, and health spas are increasing; the makers of jogging clothes and cross-country ski equipment are doing a record business; corporations are buying health programs and building fitness centers; schools and communities are sponsoring screening activities and holding health fairs.

One recent survey of American attitudes toward health showed that people are very much concerned about good health.

172

70% say that most Americans are more concerned about health than they were a few years ago.

60% do not take good health for granted.

80% welcome more openness on mental health.

79% welcome more openness on alcoholism.

80% feel they should set an example for their children on health matters.[2]

Unfortunately, this great interest in health matters has led not to a "health revolution" but to a health buying spree. People buy jogging shoes, but don't keep up their jogging; they learn relaxation techniques but don't practice them regularly; they go on diets over and over again. The study just cited came to the conclusion that "while in principle most families agree on the need for preventive health habits, few practice them in their daily lives."[3]

To review some recent statistics from a variety of studies:

- Only 12% of dieters are temporarily successful, and only 2% of these are successful in the long run.[4]

- Only ¼ of the people who started a coronary prevention program were able to maintain it.[5]

- In smoking- and weight-reduction efforts, changes are rarely maintained for longer than six months. An American Health Foundation study of 576 smokers in three different programs found that although the quit rate was 70% to 80% at the end of the program, a year later it was down to 18% to 20%.[6]

- Only 14% of motorists use seat belts—a decrease of 25% from last year, and our 55-mile-per-hour speed limit, which was saving a lot of lives, is gradually eroding.[7]

- One highly touted Finnish program designed to encourage regular physical exercise found that the program did not result in lasting

[2]Daniel Yankelovich, Florence Skelly, and Arthur White, "Family Health in an Era of Stress," Report by the Social-Research Firm of Yankelovich, Skelly, and White for General Mills, Inc., 1979.

[3]G. Dullea, "Health Survey Finds Poor Habits Prevail," *New York Times*, April 26, 1979.

[4]P. Wells, *New York Times* reporter specializing in food and nutrition, in *Cue Magazine*, November 24, 1978, p. 34.

[5]L. Scherwitz and H. Lenthal, "Strategies for Increasing Patient Compliance," *Health Values: Achieving High Level Wellness* 2, no. 6 (November–December 1978): 301–6.

[6]S. Zifferblatt and C. Wilbur, "Maintaining a Healthy Heart: Guidelines for a Feasible Goal," *Preventive Medicine* 6,(1977): 514–25.

[7]"Studies Find Decrease in Use of Seat Belts," *New York Times*, December 17, 1978, p.A–1.

modification of physical activity habits and had little effect on other life-style measures. In fact, in one of the groups studied, 48% of the people were exercising *less* after the three-year program was over.[8]

- And finally, an article in the prestigious *New England Journal of Medicine* recently reported that only 7% of the research reports appearing in eleven medical journals over a three-year period showed statistically significant results with major improvements.[9]

THE HIGH COST OF ILLNESS LIFE-STYLES

The life-styles we Americans now maintain, and the health practices we are engaged in, are costing us dearly in both dollars and in the quality and length of our lives.

The most recent statistics reported by the federal government's Center for Disease Control in Atlanta indicate that 51.3% of all deaths between the ages of 1 and 65 are the result of life-style-related factors, such as alcohol abuse, smoking, sedentary behavior, accidents, poor nutrition, and so forth.[10] Other studies show similar and even stronger correlations for most of our major diseases, such as strokes, heart attack, and cirrhosis of the liver. The cost of these life-style-related illnesses is astronomical in both human and economic terms, and it is growing substantially each year.

Illness costs in the United States last year were more than $200 billion, and some experts say that we are looking only at the most obvious expenditures. Illness is one of the major growth industries in the United States today, increasing about 18 percent per year for the past five years. It now stands just behind the housing and food industries in total dollar expenditures. If these expenditures were helping in some way to promote positive health and to stem the tide of further costs, they might be at least partially

[8] J. Ilmarinen and P. Fardy, "Physical Activity Intervention for Males with High Risk of Coronary Heart Disease: A Three-Year Followup," *Preventive Medicine* 6 (1977): 416–25.

[9] "Health Education: Panacea, Pernicious, or Pointless?" in *New England Journal of Medicine* 229, no. 13 (September 1978): 718.

[10] "Ten Leading Causes of Death in the United States 1977," Center for Disease Control, Bureau of State Services, Health Analysis and Planning for Prevention Services (Atlanta, Ga.: July 1980), section III, pp. 35–70.

defensible. Unfortunately, they are not, and the death rates from many of our life-style-related illnesses, as well as the costs, are steadily escalating.

HOW CULTURE INFLUENCES OUR HEALTH

If the interest in good health is so high and the economic cost of poor health is so great, why hasn't the "health revolution" succeeded? Why the gap between belief and practice?

Our studies and observations show that one of the major reasons is that the cultures and subcultures that exist within our society get in the way of people's ability to develop and maintain positive health practices. On the individual level, something like the following happens:

We realize that we are putting on a few too many pounds. We decide that we are really going to try to eat meals that are more nutritionally balanced. But at dinner we find that our favorite big meal has been prepared with a delicious calorie-filled dessert. Everybody else is eating, and we decide to let the war against the fat go until tomorrow.

Maybe we can cut down some calories by not joining in the coffee break at work. But one of the secretaries has a new cookie recipe and has brought some in for us to try, and anyhow the others in the department come out with some sarcasm about us working through the break to make an impression on the boss. That really got to us, and so we join the others in the cookie treat.

We decide that one *easy* way to cut out a lot of calories would be to cut way back on alcohol consumption. But at the next party, most of the other guests are drinking heavily, and it's hard to get into the swing of things unless we have a drink in our hand. So, to prove that we *are* sociable and are *not* alcoholics, we join in the drinking.

Maybe we should try exercising and not worry so much about what we eat? We'll jog every day, and that should do it. So we buy jogging shoes and jackets and set out the next morning. But it is an awful effort to get up early while everyone else is still snug in their bed. And besides, the only people who are up either honk at us impolitely to get out of the road or peek from behind their curtains as though we are something peculiar. A few even send out their dogs to bark at us.

Tensions are really getting to us. We read some books on relaxation techniques but can't seem to make this work very well. Anyhow, there are important meetings every night this week; the kids want to go to a ballgame now that baseball season is upon us; the yard work is screaming for someone to get out there and do some cultivating; and we really ought to do some further preparation on that proposal we will be taking to Chicago next week. How can a person find time to relax?

And so it goes. We have good intentions, but the tremendous influence of the culture is more than we can withstand. We end up blaming ourselves for lack of willpower and self-discipline and don't see that we are really the victims of the negative culture in which we live.

COMMUNITY ILLNESS CULTURES

On the community level, what is happening is that an illness culture has evolved. When norms in the area of health are largely negative, we can regard the culture as an illness culture, unconsciously influencing people to do things that are detrimental to their health and longevity. Whether we like it or not, our communities, for the most part, are illness cultures, encouraging sedentary habits, overuse of alcohol and drugs, poor nutrition, and high stress levels.

Cultural norms influencing our individual health practices are measurable—and when they are measured, the results are almost always startling. For example, a survey instrument called the Lifegain Health Practices Norm Indicator (see appendix E) asks people to indicate whether or not certain negative health norms exist in one or more of the groups to which they belong. From our experience using a similar norm indicator in business organizations and college classes, we expect that the number of negative health norms to be found in communities would be quite high—probably over 65 percent.

WHAT OUR COMMUNITIES CAN DO

A community of migrant workers, hired by the agricultural division of a large corporation to work in the orange groves of central Florida, was an illness culture in a most extreme form. Absenteeism was high, averaging two days a week; accident rates were double those of other industrial operations; many workers had severe chronic health problems; and their children were infested with parasitic worms and lice. Many adults had never had a medical examination. Local health facilities were not open to them; doctors in the area would not treat them. It was probably as bad a situation of public or private health as existed anywhere in the nation.

In five years that picture had remarkably improved. Migrancy was erased; substandard housing and sanitary facilities were replaced; medical and dental centers with screening, diagnostic, and treatment facilities were set up, and professional people came in to man them. Altogether the health level had been raised in a near-miraculous way.

What happened here? The people had worked together—managers, supervisors, and workers—to create a supportive environment for change. At all levels they shared hopes and fears, set goals, came to know each other as fellow human beings, and supported each other in attempts to improve their plight. Better health was only one aspect of the improvement. In terms of total wellness, there is still a long way to go, but in terms of what had been, a great deal was accomplished. What was achieved came about in the context of a caring, supportive community.

Adopting a Cultural Focus

To go beyond our present efforts and achieve a real health revolution, we will need to switch our attention from an exclusive focus on the individual to one that also focuses on the culture in which he or she lives. While it is true that as individuals we have a great deal to accomplish in changing our health practices, it is unlikely that the changes we make will maintain themselves unless we build a supportive cultural environment.

177

A data-gathering instrument called the Community-Support Indicator, a variation of the support barometer (see page 43) helps to measure the strength of support from the culture. It asks people to indicate how their communities are doing in providing support for people's efforts to improve health practices.

When approaching positive health from a cultural vantage point, a community can change its norms to support both individual and group efforts and become a powerful influence for better health. The secret of success is not to take away responsibility from the individual but to recognize that responsibility for ourselves includes responsibility for the social environment that affects us.

The reasons for our current failures in effective community health promotion programs stem not so much from an unwillingness of people to bring about change as they do from the failures of the implementation systems to cope with negative health cultures.

Our studies of factors influencing the success and failure of personal, organizational, and community change efforts suggest that the major errors of health promotion programs are associated with the lack of a culture-based participatory approach. Our experience is that people are ready and willing to participate in programs of change if they are given the opportunity to do so and that the major problems that now exist result from our inability to provide program opportunities that offer a real chance for sustained success. In health, perhaps more than in most other areas, it is important that the changes achieved are sustained over a period of time. It does little good, and perhaps some harm, to lose weight for a few months and then regain it; it does little good to jog for a few days unless it becomes a regular event.

Unfortunately, most of the programs that are currently being recommended on the community level are short-term efforts focusing only on individual change and are not likely to have continued success.

COMMON ERRORS IN
HEALTH PROMOTION

Our studies of health promotion programs indicate six traditional errors, and all of them have to do with lack of a cultural viewpoint. Briefly, these errors are the following:

- *Fragmentation of effort.* While some good programs have been developed, they are often implemented in a piecemeal fashion and their total impact minimized.
- *Overemphasis on initial motivation.* Advertising and other campaign-type efforts often bring about momentary change, but it is the maintenance of change over an extended period that has a lasting impact on positive health cultures.
- *Appeal to individual heroics.* Group-based programs are more likely to be effective than those asking people to "pull themselves up by their own bootstraps." In the long run, the programs that help people build supportive environments will influence more individuals to change.
- *Overemphasis on activities as opposed to results.* Activities such as health fairs and occasional screening programs, no matter how "successful," will have lasting value only when the changes recommended are supported by the underlying culture.
- *Undue focus on unapplied knowledge and information.* Knowledge and information, while important ingredients of a health program, are of little value if unapplied. The practical use of the knowledge in day-to-day activities needs to be emphasized.
- *A "we will do it for you" approach, rather than "together we can do it for ourselves."* People need to feel a sense of ownership of the program, which comes from their involvement in the decisions regarding it, and a responsibility for carrying it out successfully. When things are done to and for people, rather than with them, many of the worst remnants of the old illness system remain.

The basic lesson involved in all these failures is that what we do or do not do in regard to health is determined by the cultural norms of our social environments. We need to act upon the conviction that no meaningful change will be maintained without the existence of a supportive culture.

HEALTHY COMMUNITY SYSTEMS

Fortunately there now exists the technology and an approach to change that can not only help people develop life-style changes but can help them maintain them over an extended period of time. The overall approach is the Normative Systems approach to cultural change described in chapter 2. The specific health promotion program is entitled Lifegain. The Lifegain Healthy Community System is an application of Lifegain to communities. HCS is based on the same community-organizing and cultural change concepts that were used in the earlier migrant and litter projects (see the following list and figure). The system is a comprehensive one and contains guidelines that community people can use in planning and organizing their change efforts. There are educational materials that can be used with different populations, instruments for measuring progress, workshop designs, and audio-visual presentations to get people involved with the cultural framework of the program.[11]

Characteristics of an Effective Health Promotion Program
- Personal *involvement* versus leaving it to others
- *Caring* for each other versus being exclusively concerned about ourselves
- *Health* emphasis versus illness emphasis
- Basis in *sound data* versus hunches and wishful thinking
- Freedom of *choice* versus telling others what to do
- Measurable *results* versus focus on activities
- Sustained *achievement* versus campaign-type efforts
- *Systematic* approaches versus piecemeal solutions
- Positive *support* versus negative blame placing
- *Fun* and *pleasure orientation* versus grim scare tactics

All of these materials are developed in such a way that they can be tailored to particular community and organizational needs. They provide sufficient structure so that otherwise relatively untrained people can have confidence in what they are doing without their feeling that the program is so structured that it doesn't allow for individual creativity and differences.

The Providing of Guidelines

Through the system's four-phase process, community groups can analyze their own needs and resources, organize to meet those needs, implement the changes they want, evaluate their efforts, and sustain the changes over the years. While each program needs to be unique to the particular town or city, the system provides certain crucial steps that every community health promotion program needs to take, steps that have proven their value in many

[11]A Lifegain Healthy Community System Organizing Kit and related materials are available through HRI Human Resources Institute, Morristown, N.J.

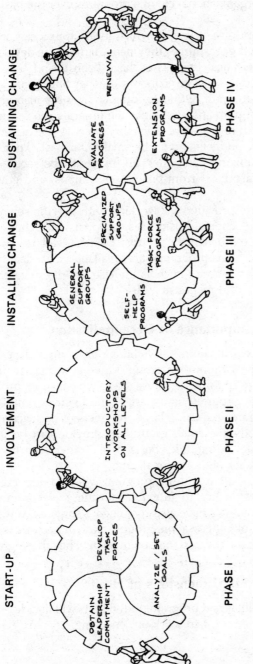

START-UP   INVOLVEMENT   INSTALLING CHANGE   SUSTAINING CHANGE

PHASE I

OBTAIN LEADERSHIP COMMITMENT

DEVELOP TASK FORCES

ANALYZE / SET GOALS

Commitment is more than lip service. It involves resources, time, budget, and personnel. Task forces are made up of volunteers. Norm instruments help in analyzing the culture and setting goals.

PHASE II

INTRODUCTORY WORKSHOPS ON ALL LEVELS

Workshops involve everyone who will be affected by the changes sought. Here people get a glimpse of the desired wellness culture and begin to see their alternatives.

PHASE III

GENERAL SUPPORT GROUPS

SPECIALIZED SUPPORT GROUPS

SELF-HELP PROGRAMS

TASK-FORCE PROGRAMS

The changes are tried out in the day-to-day activities of both the individual and the community group.

PHASE IV

EVALUATE PROGRESS

RENEWAL

EXTENSION PROGRAMS

To sustain change we need to evaluate, modify as necessary, and find ways to keep enthusiasm going.

Figure 8. The Lifegain Healthy Community Systems Model.

community and organizational change programs over the past two decades.

The system outlines ways in which local groups can secure the financial and other resources they need. Funding is developed on the local level. Local businesses have been found to be an excellent source of funds, since economically they have a good deal to gain from the program. Other funding sources are also identified during the program analysis. Since the program is a voluntary one and since much of it involves the more effective use of already existing resources, budgets should be small. Our past experience indicates that organizing personnel can frequently be secured on loan on a temporary basis from businesses, unions, and government agencies.

Guidelines are provided for working with specific segments of the community: schools, businesses, hospitals, churches, synagogues, unions, senior citizen groups, political leaders, and so on. Similarly, modular programs are available that deal with specific health practice areas, such as exercise, nutrition, cessation of smoking, safety, and responsible use of alcohol.

The Importance of Decentralization

One key to a successful community change program is decentralization. Thus, each community group, whether it be a church, business, school, or union, is encouraged to have its own individual positive health program as a part of the overall community effort. Some programs requiring larger numbers of participants or greater resources than a small group can provide can be made available on a wider community basis, while others can be conducted by the smaller organizational units.

The success of a community program will also depend to a large extent on its ability to integrate a variety of community efforts. Many individuals have already joined Y's, gyms, or weight reduction and smoking-cessation groups, and many businesses have already begun to develop their own positive health programs.

Six Dimensions of Health

Within the culturally based program, individuals will decide on the health practices they want to work on, choosing from six general

areas. A few hints about these will perhaps suggest some important changes people might want to consider.

EXERCISE AND PHYSICAL FITNESS.

Think in terms of your flexibility, strength, and endurance,
and your cardiovascular fitness. Do community residents exercise
their hearts vigorously at least twenty minutes a day four times a
week?

NUTRITION AND WEIGHT CONTROL.

Most Americans need to cut down on salt, sugar, cholesterol,
and fat; to increase the amount of fruits, vegetables, and whole
grains in their diets; and to decrease the amount of meat and
processed foods they eat.

STRESS AND STRESS MANAGEMENT.

There are many easy-to-learn relaxation exercises that, if
practiced daily, can reduce the harmful effects of stress, helping
people to avoid the perils of hypertension, heart attack, and stroke.

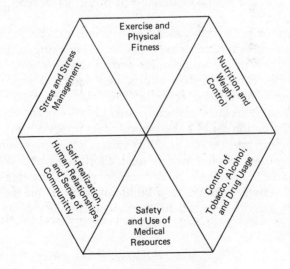

Figure 9.
The Lifegain Dimensions of
Wellness.

SAFETY AND THE PROPER USE OF
MEDICAL RESOURCES.

Do community members avoid speeding and reckless driving? Do they wear a seat belt at all times? Do they follow up on their doctor's and dentist's recommendations?

SELF-REALIZATION
AND RELATIONSHIPS
WITH OTHERS.

This area may surprise you, but think about it. Isn't wellness also a matter of good mental health, satisfying human relationships, and the fulfillment of one's potential? A recent study showed that to determine whether or not a person will die of heart disease, the best predictors are job satisfaction and overall happiness.[12]

NOT ABUSING
YOUR BODY WITH DRUGS,
ALCOHOL OR CIGARETTES.

Do you use only drugs that have been prescribed by your doctor? Do you drink moderately if at all? Have you given up smoking?

Any of these dimensions of wellness can be the focus of community action. Community task forces, working to change the health norms of the community and to develop supportive environments, can focus their efforts on a particular area—exercise and exercise norms, for example. Thus task forces might recommend changes in laws protecting the right-of-way for joggers or a school discussion series to help youngsters understand the importance of clean arteries and healthy hearts. Or they might encourage street vendors to offer health food alternatives and suggest to supermarkets that they stock more nutritious offerings. These types of activities would help build support for the good health practices individuals need to maintain if they are going to help themselves to wellness.

---

[12]*Work in America: Report of a Special Task Force to the Secretary of Health, Education and Welfare* (Cambridge, Mass.: MIT Press, 1973).

CULTURAL MEDICINE

Our health care system has evolved over the centuries, bringing medicine out of the realm of magic and superstition into the realm of scientific and technological marvels. More recently there is a growing realization that prevention and life-style changes need more attention. Now we suggest an additional dimension: the next step in the evolution of health, we believe, is cultural medicine.

It is tragic to think that the communities that we have created to better our lives are serving to destroy them. Fortunately, it doesn't have to be that way. It really is possible to apply cultural medicine to our communities and to change them into the kind of wellness cultures we need for greater personal health and longevity.

chapter fourteen
Shaping Our Future and Ourselves

"Realistic hope," Karl Menninger once said, "is based on the attempt to understand the concrete conditions of reality, to see one's role in it realistically, and to engage in such efforts of thoughtful action as might be expected to bring about the hoped-for change."[1] Once people have become aware of the organizational unconscious and understood their roles in facilitating cultural change, they have exciting prospects of "thoughtful action" ahead. This book is intended to contribute to that process.

By presenting our particular system for making and sustaining positive change, we do not mean to claim a cure-all for the world's ills. Changing things demands on ongoing process, not a fixed blueprint for all eventualities. Sustained change requires commitment, hard work, creativity, and continuing renewal efforts, but the rewards are great. The method espoused here doesn't work every time (what does?), but it works more often than anything we know of.

Charles Reich in his *Greening of America*[2] offered a romantic vision of the transformation of society into a more humanistic environment. We suggest a way to achieve that vision of a greater humanity in our organizations and communities—a way that

[1]Karl Menninger, *Vital Balance: The Life Process in Mental Health and Illness* (New York: Penguin, 1977), p. 399.
[2]Charles Reich, *Greening of America* (New York: Random House, 1970).

involves hard work and takes into account the cultural realities of our situation. For the "greening of America" we offer a pick and a shovel—and a flexible, ongoing, participative process.

Creating and maintaining the changes we want in our organizational cultures will not be easy, but it is as possible as it is exciting. And the rewards begin as soon as we begin to get involved and start to feel the satisfaction and hopefulness of being masters rather than victims of our environments.

We can never be free of the cultures that we live in—nor would we want to be—for the socializing forces of our cultures are part of what make us human. But we can extricate ourselves from the culture's tyranny and become better able to control our lives. Increased consciousness of the culture's power makes it possible for us to deal with it. A systematic, culture-based process helps us realize the changes we want, adding to our own individuality and effectiveness and to the individuality and effectiveness of our organizations. In this way we become more capable of shaping our future and ourselves.

Appendixes

The Organizational Leadership
Development Module (OLDM) System

This system provides individual and group self-instructional programs on key areas of organizational concern. Materials used in this system include the following:*

AN OVERVIEW OF THE LEADERSHIP
DEVELOPMENT SYSTEM.

This booklet explains the Leadership Development System as a part of a systematic cultural change program. It describes the different materials of the series and how to implement the program for cultural change effectively. An appendix includes a program design for the module introductory session, a sample meeting schedule, and a list of the module components.

SYSTEMS MANUAL FOR THE IMPLEMENTATION
OF THE ORGANIZATIONAL LEADERSHIP
DEVELOPMENT MODULES.

This manual describes the Organizational Leadership Development Module system for normative change. The manual contains the rationale as well as the step-by-step process to modify and strengthen the cultural influences upon leadership. The manual consists of two major parts. The first section is general and includes a description of the OLDM and detailed instructions for

*For a price list, order blank, and additional information regarding the OLDM system materials discussed, write to: HRI Human Resources Institute, Tempe Wick Road, Morristown, New Jersey 07960.

their systematic implementation in an organizational setting. The second part of this manual is an appendix that consists of normative instruments, sample materials, charts, and forms used in understanding and implementing the OLDM system.

TRAINER/COACH MANUAL.

This manual is a skills-training guide and an orientation to the entire Organizational Leadership Development module system. The components of the modules are explained, followed by suggestions on how to present it to a group as well as how to follow up on the job.

INTRODUCTION TO MODULE UNITS.

This booklet explains the basic concepts of and process for cultural change. It describes the implementation of the OLDM System and the different modules, including module components.

ELEMENTS OF LEADERSHIP.

This module identifies effective leaders as those who demonstrate maximum concern for both people and results. It explains how such leadership contributes to a healthy and productive organizational culture. In addition to the content presentation, it includes the basic components of a content quiz and summary, a goal-setting booklet, a booklet of practice and demonstration experiences, and a checklist for action.

PERFORMANCE PLANNING AND REVIEW.

This module explains how to build effective organizational cultures by keeping a clear and consistent focus on individuals as well as work team results. In addition to the content presentation, the module includes the basic module components of a content quiz and summary, a goal-setting booklet, a booklet of practice and demonstration experiences, and a checklist for action.

EXCELLENCE IN MANAGING PEOPLE
THROUGH PERFORMANCE APPRAISAL.

This module defines the four phases of performance appraisal as a process and explains how successful managers are those who continually face the problems of meeting corporate goals and simultaneously motivate, encourage, develop, reward, satisfy, support, and confront their employees. In addition to the content presentation, the module includes the basic components of a content quiz and summary, a goal-setting booklet, a booklet of practice and demonstration experiences, and a checklist for action.

THE ASSUMPTION OF RESPONSIBILITY.

This module explains how organizational cultures are positively affected when people openly accept responsibility for what happens. In addition to the content presentation, the module includes the basic components of a content quiz and summary, a goal-setting booklet, a booklet of practice and demonstration experiences, and a checklist for action.

ORGANIZATIONAL POLICIES AND PROCEDURES.

This module defines *policies* as the organization's general direction, and *goals* and *procedures* as the general guidelines for getting there. It also explains how they can help people and organizations to work more effectively. In addition to the content presentation, the module includes the basic components of a content quiz and summary, a goal-setting booklet, a booklet of practice and demonstration experiences, and a checklist for action.

SUPPORT AND CONFRONTATION.

This module explains how effective people at all levels can directly influence organizational norms by firmly supporting positive behavior and directly confronting negative behavior. In addition to the content presentation, the module includes the basic components of a content quiz and summary, a goal-setting booklet, a booklet of practice and demonstration experiences, and a checklist for action.

EFFECTIVE WORK TEAM MEETINGS.

This module defines what work team meetings are, how they work, and what they can and cannot accomplish. In addition to the content presentation, the module includes the basic components of a content quiz and summary, a goal-setting booklet, a booklet of practice and demonstration experiences, and a checklist for action.

INVOLVEMENT AND MOTIVATION.

This module explains how involvement and motivation can create cultures that turn people either on or off. In addition to the content presentation, the module includes the basic components of a content quiz and summary, a goal-setting booklet, a booklet of practice and demonstration experiences, and a checklist for action.

COMMUNICATION AND INFORMATION SYSTEMS.

This module explains what effective communication is and how it relates to the skills of leadership. It also defines the four information systems and their importance to work teams. In addition to the content presentation, the module includes the basic components of a content quiz and summary, a goal-setting booklet, a booklet of practice and demonstration experiences, and a checklist for action.

TRAIN THE TRAINERS.

This module consists of individual articles that represent the basic concepts of being an effective trainer. It covers an approach to motivation, what to observe in groups, how to create a good atmosphere for learning and the use of materials. In addition to the content presentation, the module includes the basic components of a goal-setting booklet, a booklet of practice and demonstration experiences, and a checklist for action.

MANAGEMENT-BY-OBJECTIVES.

This module first presents what management-by-objectives is, how it works, and why it is important to everyone; secondly, it presents methods of setting measurable objectives, developing action plans, and measuring actual results. The module also includes the basic components contained in other OLDM modules.

ORGANIZATIONAL PROBLEM SOLVING.

This module presents ten specific guidelines for effective problem solving that can help people become more effective organizational leaders. These guidelines are then applied to a systematic process that enables people to analyze, assess, and activate a solution. The module also includes the basic components contained in other OLDM modules.

ORIENTATION.

This module presents the elements of orientation with a complete discussion of the two necessary components of a successful orientation system. The first is the individual effort of each supervisor every time he or she welcomes a new associate; and the second is the company-wide effort that supplements the supervisor's efforts and provides new associates with training, materials, and an orientation to give them the information necessary for a well-rounded program. The module also includes the basic components contained in other OLDM modules.

APPENDIX B

"AS I SEE IT..."
A Norm Indicator for Organizations

Directions

One of the most important characteristics of all groups or organizations is the pattern of norms that tends to develop within them. This survey is designed to help identify some of the key norms that may or may not exist in your group or organization. The results of this survey can be useful in planning for improvement.

A norm is what's expected or supported within a group or organization. Norms are really "the way things are," not necessarily the way we would like them to be. Often these unwritten rules or norms of the organization go against the official rules and policies that have been established.

STEP I.

Following the directions and sample statements is a list of possible norms that may or may not exist in your group or organization.* We would like you to indicate your level of agreement or disagreement with each statement by placing an X in the appropriate box on the answer sheet. If you change your mind after you have marked a response, blacken out your old response and mark your new response with an X.

*Survey statements, answer sheets, and scoring keys contained in Appendix B and Appendix C, Copyright 1975 by HRI Human Resources Institute.

STEP II.

After you have indicated with an X your level of agreement with each statement, please circle the response that is closest to the response that you would prefer to be true and that you think would be most helpful in terms of organizational effectiveness.

In order to see if you have the hang of it, read each of the following statements and check to see if the answer is the same as the one you would have chosen for your organization.

	STRONGLY AGREE	AGREE	UNDECIDED	DISAGREE	STRONGLY DISAGREE
As I see it, it is a norm around here in our organization...					
a. for people to wear clothes to work	(X)	( )	( )	( )	( )
b. for people to shoot people when they disagree with them	( )	( )	( )	( )	(X)
c. for people not to care how much money they earn	( )	( )	( )	( )	(X)

Are the answers the same as the ones you would have given? If they are not, you are either a member of a very unusual organization or you should ask for some clarification of this survey. Mark your responses to the following statements on the answer sheet (see p. 197).

As I See It, It Is a Norm Around Here In Our Organization...

1. for people to feel "turned on" and enthusiastic about what they're doing
2. for individual and organizational goals to be in harmony with one another
3. for teamwork to be neglected
4. for organizational policies and procedures to be helpful, well understood, and up-to-date
5. for people to communicate well with one another

As I See It, It Is a Norm Around Here In Our Organization...

6. for people to point out errors in a way that's constructive and helpful
7. for people to blame other people for their own mistakes
8. for people to feel they can only succeed at the expense of others
9. for groups to function without clear goals and objectives
10. for resources to be organized and time to be scheduled effectively
11. for managers to neglect individual capabilities, wants, and needs in making job assignments
12. for people to get whatever training is needed to help them succeed in their work
13. for people to avoid making decisions and allow problems to become chronic
14. to measure for the organization's specific results
15. to maintain the progress that is made
16. for change efforts to be based on sound information
17. for leaders to fail to practice what they preach
18. for people to care about and strive for excellent performance
19. for people to approach change efforts haphazardly without taking into account all the important factors
20. for leaders to make a strong effort to involve and motivate people in their work
21. for people not to have any way of measuring how well they are doing
22. for people to work together effectively
23. for organizational policies and procedures to get in the way of what people are trying to accomplish
24. for people to seek out the ideas and opinions of others actively
25. for people to be recognized and rewarded for excellent performance
26. for people to feel responsible for doing their own job right so that the whole team succeeds
27. for people to help each other when they are having difficulty
28. for groups to define goals clearly before a task is begun
29. for needless duplication of effort to occur
30. for selection and promotion practices to be fair and equitable
31. for training needs to be neglected
32. to look for solutions to problems from which all people will benefit, rather than solutions from which some win and some lose
33. to focus on effort or talk rather than on results
34. for leaders to be too busy to follow up on jobs they've assigned to people
35. for people to avoid blame placing and instead look for constructive approaches to change
36. for leaders to be concerned equally about both people and production issues

37. for people to care about doing their best
38. for people to approach change by dealing with the cause of problems, not just the symptoms
39. for people to feel "turned off" by their work in the organization
40. for people to get feedback on how they're doing so that they can develop as individuals in a planned way
41. for each person to have an opportunity to be a member of a functioning, effective work team
42. to review organizational policies and procedures regularly and make changes when they are needed
43. for people to practice effective two-way communications
44. for people to confront negative behavior or norms constructively
45. for people to assume responsibility for things that go wrong in their work groups
46. for people to treat each other as people and not just "a pair of hands"
47. for the goals of the organization to be clear and well communicated
48. for some people to be overworked while others have nothing to do
49. for job assignments to be made on a hit-or-miss basis rather than through a systematic process
50. for new people to be oriented to the job properly
51. for decisions to be made in a haphazard way
52. for leaders to help their work team members succeed
53. for improvements to be temporary and not lasting
54. for people involved in change efforts to focus on promises rather than on results
55. for leaders to try to improve their leadership
56. for people to take pride in their own work and the work of their organization
57. for people to follow through on programs that they begin
58. for people to feel really involved in the work of the organization
59. for people to plan their work goals and review progress toward their accomplishment regularly
60. for people who work together to meet regularly to deal with important issues and to focus on ways of improving performance
61. for people to view policies and procedures as things to be worked around or avoided
62. for people to need more information than they have in order to do a good job
63. for leaders not to notice what people do unless they do it wrong
64. for people to assume responsibility for what happens in the organization
65. for people to give and receive feedback in helpful ways

As I See It, It Is a Norm Around Here In Our Organization . . .

66. for people to know exactly what their job requires
67. for a leader to make the best use of the work time available in his or her group
68. for selection and promotion practices to be prejudiced against women or minority groups
69. for new people to have to "sink or swim" in learning their job
70. when something goes wrong, to blame someone rather than doing something about it
71. for people to get regular feedback on how well their work team and organization are doing in meeting their objectives
72. for people to start things without following through
73. for people to understand what it really takes to improve things in an organization
74. for leaders to demonstrate their own commitment to what the organization is trying to accomplish
75. for people to be satisfied with less than their best performance
76. for people to be directly involved in the development of changes affecting them
77. for more attention to be given to failures and mistakes than to successes and correct actions
78. for a spirit of cooperation and teamwork to be felt throughout the organization
79. for people to focus on activities and problems rather than on the results to be achieved
80. for a rivalry to exist among groups within the organization that gets in the way of achieving results
81. for people to work together as positive and effective teams for getting the job done well
82. for people to emphasize the negative rather than the positive in assessing performance
83. for people who work together to meet only rarely to discuss how their work is going and how it can be improved
84. for every effort to be made to assure that people have many success experiences

Norm Indicator
for Organizations
Answer Sheet

Scoring Directions: Add up the total score using the scoring key following this answer sheet. The highest possible score, indicating the greatest number of positive norms, is 256. The lowest score possible is 0.

Name _____   Date _____

	STRONGLY AGREE	AGREE	UNDECIDED	DISAGREE	STRONGLY DISAGREE			STRONGLY AGREE	AGREE	UNDECIDED	DISAGREE	STRONGLY DISAGREE
1.	( )	( )	( )	( )	( )		43.	( )	( )	( )	( )	( )
2.	( )	( )	( )	( )	( )		44.	( )	( )	( )	( )	( )
3.	( )	( )	( )	( )	( )		45.	( )	( )	( )	( )	( )
4.	( )	( )	( )	( )	( )		46.	( )	( )	( )	( )	( )
5.	( )	( )	( )	( )	( )		47.	( )	( )	( )	( )	( )
6.	( )	( )	( )	( )	( )		48.	( )	( )	( )	( )	( )
7.	( )	( )	( )	( )	( )		49.	( )	( )	( )	( )	( )
8.	( )	( )	( )	( )	( )		50.	( )	( )	( )	( )	( )
9.	( )	( )	( )	( )	( )		51.	( )	( )	( )	( )	( )
10.	( )	( )	( )	( )	( )		52.	( )	( )	( )	( )	( )
11.	( )	( )	( )	( )	( )		53.	( )	( )	( )	( )	( )
12.	( )	( )	( )	( )	( )		54.	( )	( )	( )	( )	( )
13.	( )	( )	( )	( )	( )		55.	( )	( )	( )	( )	( )
14.	( )	( )	( )	( )	( )		56.	( )	( )	( )	( )	( )
15.	( )	( )	( )	( )	( )		57.	( )	( )	( )	( )	( )
16.	( )	( )	( )	( )	( )		58.	( )	( )	( )	( )	( )
17.	( )	( )	( )	( )	( )		59.	( )	( )	( )	( )	( )
18.	( )	( )	( )	( )	( )		60.	( )	( )	( )	( )	( )
19.	( )	( )	( )	( )	( )		61.	( )	( )	( )	( )	( )
20.	( )	( )	( )	( )	( )		62.	( )	( )	( )	( )	( )
21.	( )	( )	( )	( )	( )		63.	( )	( )	( )	( )	( )
22.	( )	( )	( )	( )	( )		64.	( )	( )	( )	( )	( )
23.	( )	( )	( )	( )	( )		65.	( )	( )	( )	( )	( )
24.	( )	( )	( )	( )	( )		66.	( )	( )	( )	( )	( )
25.	( )	( )	( )	( )	( )		67.	( )	( )	( )	( )	( )
26.	( )	( )	( )	( )	( )		68.	( )	( )	( )	( )	( )
27.	( )	( )	( )	( )	( )		69.	( )	( )	( )	( )	( )
28.	( )	( )	( )	( )	( )		70.	( )	( )	( )	( )	( )
29.	( )	( )	( )	( )	( )		71.	( )	( )	( )	( )	( )
30.	( )	( )	( )	( )	( )		72.	( )	( )	( )	( )	( )
31.	( )	( )	( )	( )	( )		73.	( )	( )	( )	( )	( )

	STRONGLY AGREE	AGREE	UNDECIDED	DISAGREE	STRONGLY DISAGREE		STRONGLY AGREE	AGREE	UNDECIDED	DISAGREE	STRONGLY DISAGREE
32.	( )	( )	( )	( )	( )	74.	( )	( )	( )	( )	( )
33.	( )	( )	( )	( )	( )	75.	( )	( )	( )	( )	( )
34.	( )	( )	( )	( )	( )	76.	( )	( )	( )	( )	( )
35.	( )	( )	( )	( )	( )	77.	( )	( )	( )	( )	( )
36.	( )	( )	( )	( )	( )	78.	( )	( )	( )	( )	( )
37.	( )	( )	( )	( )	( )	79.	( )	( )	( )	( )	( )
38.	( )	( )	( )	( )	( )	80.	( )	( )	( )	( )	( )
39.	( )	( )	( )	( )	( )	81.	( )	( )	( )	( )	( )
40.	( )	( )	( )	( )	( )	82.	( )	( )	( )	( )	( )
41.	( )	( )	( )	( )	( )	83.	( )	( )	( )	( )	( )
42.	( )	( )	( )	( )	( )	84.	( )	( )	( )	( )	( )

Norm Indicator
for Organizations
Scoring Key

Name _____   Date _____

	STRONGLY AGREE	AGREE	UNDECIDED	DISAGREE	STRONGLY DISAGREE		STRONGLY AGREE	AGREE	UNDECIDED	DISAGREE	STRONGLY DISAGREE
1.	(4)	(3)	(2)	(1)	(0)	43.	(4)	(3)	(2)	(1)	(0)
2.	(4)	(3)	(2)	(1)	(0)	44.	(4)	(3)	(2)	(1)	(0)
3.	(0)	(1)	(2)	(3)	(4)	45.	(4)	(3)	(2)	(1)	(0)
4.	(4)	(3)	(2)	(1)	(0)	46.	(4)	(3)	(2)	(1)	(0)
5.	(4)	(3)	(2)	(1)	(0)	47.	(4)	(3)	(2)	(1)	(0)
6.	(4)	(3)	(2)	(1)	(0)	48.	(0)	(1)	(2)	(3)	(4)
7.	(0)	(1)	(2)	(3)	(4)	49.	(0)	(1)	(2)	(3)	(4)
8.	(0)	(1)	(2)	(3)	(4)	50.	(4)	(3)	(2)	(1)	(0)

	STRONGLY AGREE	AGREE	UNDECIDED	DISAGREE	STRONGLY DISAGREE		STRONGLY AGREE	AGREE	UNDECIDED	DISAGREE	STRONGLY DISAGREE
9.	(0)	(1)	(2)	(3)	(4)	51.	(0)	(1)	(2)	(3)	(4)
10.	(4)	(3)	(2)	(1)	(0)	52.	(4)	(3)	(2)	(1)	(0)
11.	(0)	(1)	(2)	(3)	(4)	53.	(0)	(1)	(2)	(3)	(4)
12.	(4)	(3)	(2)	(1)	(0)	54.	(0)	(1)	(2)	(3)	(4)
13.	(0)	(1)	(2)	(3)	(4)	55.	(4)	(3)	(2)	(1)	(0)
14.	(4)	(3)	(2)	(1)	(0)	56.	(4)	(3)	(2)	(1)	(0)
15.	(4)	(3)	(2)	(1)	(0)	57.	(4)	(3)	(2)	(1)	(0)
16.	(4)	(3)	(2)	(1)	(0)	58.	(4)	(3)	(2)	(1)	(0)
17.	(0)	(1)	(2)	(3)	(4)	59.	(4)	(3)	(2)	(1)	(0)
18.	(4)	(3)	(2)	(1)	(0)	60.	(4)	(3)	(2)	(1)	(0)
19.	(0)	(1)	(2)	(3)	(4)	61.	(0)	(1)	(2)	(3)	(4)
20.	(4)	(3)	(2)	(1)	(0)	62.	(0)	(1)	(2)	(3)	(4)
21.	(0)	(1)	(2)	(3)	(4)	63.	(0)	(1)	(2)	(3)	(4)
22.	(4)	(3)	(2)	(1)	(0)	64.	(4)	(3)	(2)	(1)	(0)
23.	(0)	(1)	(2)	(3)	(4)	65.	(4)	(3)	(2)	(1)	(0)
24.	(4)	(3)	(2)	(1)	(0)	66.	(4)	(3)	(2)	(1)	(0)
25.	(4)	(3)	(2)	(1)	(0)	67.	(4)	(3)	(2)	(1)	(0)
26.	(4)	(3)	(2)	(1)	(0)	68.	(0)	(1)	(2)	(3)	(4)
27.	(4)	(3)	(2)	(1)	(0)	69.	(0)	(1)	(2)	(3)	(4)
28.	(4)	(3)	(2)	(1)	(0)	70.	(0)	(1)	(2)	(3)	(4)
29.	(0)	(1)	(2)	(3)	(4)	71.	(4)	(3)	(2)	(1)	(0)
30.	(4)	(3)	(2)	(1)	(0)	72.	(0)	(1)	(2)	(3)	(4)
31.	(0)	(1)	(2)	(3)	(4)	73.	(4)	(3)	(2)	(1)	(0)
32.	(4)	(3)	(2)	(1)	(0)	74.	(4)	(3)	(2)	(1)	(0)
33.	(0)	(1)	(2)	(3)	(4)	75.	(0)	(1)	(2)	(3)	(4)
34.	(0)	(1)	(2)	(3)	(4)	76.	(4)	(3)	(2)	(1)	(0)
35.	(4)	(3)	(2)	(1)	(0)	77.	(0)	(1)	(2)	(3)	(4)
36.	(4)	(3)	(2)	(1)	(0)	78.	(4)	(3)	(2)	(1)	(0)
37.	(4)	(3)	(2)	(1)	(0)	79.	(0)	(1)	(2)	(3)	(4)
38.	(4)	(3)	(2)	(1)	(0)	80.	(0)	(1)	(2)	(3)	(4)
39.	(0)	(1)	(2)	(3)	(4)	81.	(4)	(3)	(2)	(1)	(0)
40.	(4)	(3)	(2)	(1)	(0)	82.	(0)	(1)	(2)	(3)	(4)
41.	(4)	(3)	(2)	(1)	(0)	83.	(0)	(1)	(2)	(3)	(4)
42.	(4)	(3)	(2)	(1)	(0)	84.	(4)	(3)	(2)	(1)	(0)

APPENDIX C

"AS I SEE IT..."
A Norm Indicator on Leadership

Directions

One of the most important characteristics of all groups or organizations is the pattern of norms that tends to develop within them. This survey is designed to help identify some of the key norms that may or may not exist in your group or organization. The results of this survey can be useful in planning for improvement and change.

A norm is what's expected or supported within a group or organization. Norms are really "the way things are," not necessarily the way we would like them to be. Often these unwritten rules or norms of the organization go against the official rules and policies that have been established.

STEP I.

Following the directions and sample statements is a list of possible norms that may or may not exist in your group or organization. We would like you to indicate your level of agreement or disagreement with each statement by placing an X in the appropriate box on the answer sheet. If you change your mind after you have marked a response, black out your old response and mark your new response with an X.

STEP II.

After you have indicated with an X your level of agreement with whether or not that norm now exists within your organization, please circle the response that is closest to the response that you would prefer to be true and that you think would be most helpful in terms of organizational effectiveness.

In order to see if you have the hang of it, read each of the following statements and check to see if the answer is the same as the one you would have chosen for your organization.

	STRONGLY AGREE	AGREE	UNDECIDED	DISAGREE	STRONGLY DISAGREE
As I see it, it is a norm around here in our organization...					
a. for people to wear clothes to work	(X)	( )	( )	( )	( )
b. for people to shoot people when they disagree with them	( )	( )	( )	( )	(X)
c. for people not to care how much money they earn	( )	( )	( )	( )	(X)

Are the answers the same as the ones you would have given? If they are not, you are either a member of a very unusual organization or you should ask for some clarification about this survey. Mark your responses to the following statements on the answer sheet (see p. 205).

As I see it, it is a norm around here in our organization...

1. for leaders to make sure that people get whatever training is needed to help them succeed in their work
2. for leaders to be concerned fully about both people and job achievement
3. for leaders to avoid making decisions and to allow problems to become chronic
4. for leaders to contribute to a spirit of cooperation and teamwork throughout the organization
5. for leaders to make sure that organizational policies and procedures are helpful, well-understood, and up-to-date
6. for leaders to make sure that people help each other when they are having difficulty
7. for leaders to neglect individual capabilities, wants, and needs in making job assignments
8. for people who work together to meet rarely in order to discuss how their work is going and how it can be improved
9. for groups to function without clear goals and objectives
10. for leaders to organize and schedule time and resources effectively

As I see it, it is a norm around here in our organization . . .

11. for leaders not to notice what people do unless they do it wrong
12. for leaders to communicate well with those they supervise
13. for leaders to be satisfied with mediocre or routine performance
14. for leaders to have a clear way of measuring results
15. for leaders to ensure proper follow-through in planning and implementation of work assignments
16. for leaders to see that change efforts are based on sound information
17. for leaders to see performance review as a once- or twice-a-year activity
18. for leaders to make sure that people feel "turned on" and enthusiastic about what they're doing
19. for leaders to approach change efforts haphazardly without taking into account all the important factors
20. for leaders to make sure that new people are properly oriented to the job
21. for leaders to fail to practice what they preach
22. for leaders to concentrate on solutions to problems rather than on placing blame
23. for leaders to neglect teamwork
24. for leaders to review organizational policies and procedures regularly and to make changes when they are needed
25. for leaders to treat those they supervise as people and not just "a pair of hands"
26. for leaders to use effective selection procedures when employing new people or filling new job assignments
27. for leaders to make sure that each person has an opportunity to be a member of a functioning, effective work team
28. for leaders to be clear about what they are trying to accomplish
29. for leaders to allow needless duplication of effort to occur
30. for leaders to be constructive and helpful when they point out errors and mistakes
31. for leaders to practice one-way rather than two-way communication with those they supervise
32. for leaders to care about and strive for excellent performance
33. for leaders to focus on effort or talk rather than on results
34. for leaders to be too busy to follow up on jobs they've assigned to people
35. for leaders to avoid blame placing and instead look for constructive approaches to change
36. for leaders to assure the maximum development of each person they supervise

37. for leaders to involve those they supervise in setting their own work objectives and work methods
38. for leaders to approach change by dealing with the real causes of problems and not just the symptoms
39. for leaders to neglect training needs
40. for leaders to try continually to improve their leadership skills
41. for leaders to feel responsible for helping the whole team succeed
42. for leaders to help those they supervise to work together effectively
43. for leaders to see that policies and procedures are used constructively to further the work of the organization
44. for leaders to give and receive feedback in a helpful way
45. for leaders to be systematic in making job assignments
46. for leaders to hold regular and effective meetings of their work team
47. for leaders to help people to define goals and tasks clearly
48. for leaders to allow some people to be overworked while others have nothing to do
49. for leaders not to recognize and reward those they supervise for excellent performance
50. for leaders to seek out actively the ideas and opinions of those they supervise
51. for leaders to lack high performance standards
52. for leaders to build a positive success orientation within their work team
53. for leaders to focus on short-term, temporary improvements rather than on long-term, permanent solutions
54. for leaders involved in change efforts to focus on promises rather than on results
55. for leaders to provide those they supervise with regular feedback on how they're doing
56. for leaders to feel really involved in the work of the organization
57. for leaders to follow through on programs that they begin
58. for leaders to avoid "sink or swim" approaches to the development and training of new people
59. for leaders to demonstrate their own commitment to what the organization is trying to accomplish
60. for leaders to view leadership responsibility as something to be shared
61. for leaders to encourage the development of a rivalry between groups that gets in the way of achieving results
62. for leaders to allow organizational policies and procedures to get in the way of what people are trying to accomplish

As I see it, it is a norm around here in our organization . . .

63. for leaders to encourage win-lose competition within the work team or organization

64. for leaders to help maximize the potential of women or minority group members

65. for leaders to make sure that they and their work teams get together regularly to set goals and review progress toward their achievement

66. for leaders to make sure that people know exactly what their jobs require

67. for leaders to make the best use of the work time available in their work groups

68. for leaders to confront negative behavior by putting people down

69. for leaders to fail to see that those they supervise have the information they need to do a good job

70. for leaders to do little to help those they supervise take pride in their work and the work of the organization

71. for leaders to make sure that people get regular feedback on how well their work team and organization are doing in meeting their objectives

72. for leaders to encourage those they supervise to start things without following through

73. for leaders to assure proper planning, implementation, and follow-through in change efforts

74. for leaders to implement an effective system for planning and reviewing the performance of each person they supervise

75. for people to feel "turned off" by their work in the organization

76. for leaders to involve people directly in the development of changes affecting them

77. for leaders to give more attention to failures and mistakes than to successes and correct actions

78. for leaders to try to solve problems rather than complaining about them

79. for leaders to focus on activities and problems rather than on the results to be achieved

80. for leaders to make decisions in a haphazard way

81. for leaders to assume responsibility for what happens in the organization

82. for leaders to emphasize the negative rather than the positive in assessing performance

83. for leaders to blame other people for their own mistakes

84. for leaders to make every effort to ensure that those they supervise have many success experiences

Leadership
Norm Indicator
Answer Sheet

Scoring Directions: Add up the total score using the scoring key following this answer sheet. The highest possible score, indicating the greatest number of positive norms, is 256. The lowest score possible is 0.

Name _____

Position _____

Date _____

Organization or Division _____

	STRONGLY AGREE	AGREE	UNDECIDED	DISAGREE	STRONGLY DISAGREE		STRONGLY AGREE	AGREE	UNDECIDED	DISAGREE	STRONGLY DISAGREE
1.	( )	( )	( )	( )	( )	43.	( )	( )	( )	( )	( )
2.	( )	( )	( )	( )	( )	44.	( )	( )	( )	( )	( )
3.	( )	( )	( )	( )	( )	45.	( )	( )	( )	( )	( )
4.	( )	( )	( )	( )	( )	46.	( )	( )	( )	( )	( )
5.	( )	( )	( )	( )	( )	47.	( )	( )	( )	( )	( )
6.	( )	( )	( )	( )	( )	48.	( )	( )	( )	( )	( )
7.	( )	( )	( )	( )	( )	49.	( )	( )	( )	( )	( )
8.	( )	( )	( )	( )	( )	50.	( )	( )	( )	( )	( )
9.	( )	( )	( )	( )	( )	51.	( )	( )	( )	( )	( )
10.	( )	( )	( )	( )	( )	52.	( )	( )	( )	( )	( )
11.	( )	( )	( )	( )	( )	53.	( )	( )	( )	( )	( )
12.	( )	( )	( )	( )	( )	54.	( )	( )	( )	( )	( )
13.	( )	( )	( )	( )	( )	55.	( )	( )	( )	( )	( )
14.	( )	( )	( )	( )	( )	56.	( )	( )	( )	( )	( )
15.	( )	( )	( )	( )	( )	57.	( )	( )	( )	( )	( )
16.	( )	( )	( )	( )	( )	58.	( )	( )	( )	( )	( )
17.	( )	( )	( )	( )	( )	59.	( )	( )	( )	( )	( )
18.	( )	( )	( )	( )	( )	60.	( )	( )	( )	( )	( )
19.	( )	( )	( )	( )	( )	61.	( )	( )	( )	( )	( )

	STRONGLY AGREE	AGREE	UNDECIDED	DISAGREE	STRONGLY DISAGREE			STRONGLY AGREE	AGREE	UNDECIDED	DISAGREE	STRONGLY DISAGREE
20.	( )	( )	( )	( )	( )		62.	( )	( )	( )	( )	( )
21.	( )	( )	( )	( )	( )		63.	( )	( )	( )	( )	( )
22.	( )	( )	( )	( )	( )		64.	( )	( )	( )	( )	( )
23.	( )	( )	( )	( )	( )		65.	( )	( )	( )	( )	( )
24.	( )	( )	( )	( )	( )		66.	( )	( )	( )	( )	( )
25.	( )	( )	( )	( )	( )		67.	( )	( )	( )	( )	( )
26.	( )	( )	( )	( )	( )		68.	( )	( )	( )	( )	( )
27.	( )	( )	( )	( )	( )		69.	( )	( )	( )	( )	( )
28.	( )	( )	( )	( )	( )		70.	( )	( )	( )	( )	( )
29.	( )	( )	( )	( )	( )		71.	( )	( )	( )	( )	( )
30.	( )	( )	( )	( )	( )		72.	( )	( )	( )	( )	( )
31.	( )	( )	( )	( )	( )		73.	( )	( )	( )	( )	( )
32.	( )	( )	( )	( )	( )		74.	( )	( )	( )	( )	( )
33.	( )	( )	( )	( )	( )		75.	( )	( )	( )	( )	( )
34.	( )	( )	( )	( )	( )		76.	( )	( )	( )	( )	( )
35.	( )	( )	( )	( )	( )		77.	( )	( )	( )	( )	( )
36.	( )	( )	( )	( )	( )		78.	( )	( )	( )	( )	( )
37.	( )	( )	( )	( )	( )		79.	( )	( )	( )	( )	( )
38.	( )	( )	( )	( )	( )		80.	( )	( )	( )	( )	( )
39.	( )	( )	( )	( )	( )		81.	( )	( )	( )	( )	( )
40.	( )	( )	( )	( )	( )		82.	( )	( )	( )	( )	( )
41.	( )	( )	( )	( )	( )		83.	( )	( )	( )	( )	( )
42.	( )	( )	( )	( )	( )		84.	( )	( )	( )	( )	( )

Leadership
Norm Indicator
Scoring Key

Name _____

Position _____

Date _____

Organization or Division _____

206

	STRONGLY AGREE	AGREE	UNDECIDED	DISAGREE	STRONGLY DISAGREE		STRONGLY AGREE	AGREE	UNDECIDED	DISAGREE	STRONGLY DISAGREE
1.	(4)	(3)	(2)	(1)	(0)	43.	(4)	(3)	(2)	(1)	(0)
2.	(4)	(3)	(2)	(1)	(0)	44.	(4)	(3)	(2)	(1)	(0)
3.	(0)	(1)	(2)	(3)	(4)	45.	(4)	(3)	(2)	(1)	(0)
4.	(4)	(3)	(2)	(1)	(0)	46.	(4)	(3)	(2)	(1)	(0)
5.	(4)	(3)	(2)	(1)	(0)	47.	(4)	(3)	(2)	(1)	(0)
6.	(4)	(3)	(2)	(1)	(0)	48.	(0)	(1)	(2)	(3)	(4)
7.	(0)	(1)	(2)	(3)	(4)	49.	(0)	(1)	(2)	(3)	(4)
8.	(0)	(1)	(2)	(3)	(4)	50.	(4)	(3)	(2)	(1)	(0)
9.	(0)	(1)	(2)	(3)	(4)	51.	(0)	(1)	(2)	(3)	(4)
10.	(4)	(3)	(2)	(1)	(0)	52.	(4)	(3)	(2)	(1)	(0)
11.	(0)	(1)	(2)	(3)	(4)	53.	(0)	(1)	(2)	(3)	(4)
12.	(4)	(3)	(2)	(1)	(0)	54.	(0)	(1)	(2)	(3)	(4)
13.	(0)	(1)	(2)	(3)	(4)	55.	(4)	(3)	(2)	(1)	(0)
14.	(4)	(3)	(2)	(1)	(0)	56.	(4)	(3)	(2)	(1)	(0)
15.	(4)	(3)	(2)	(1)	(0)	57.	(4)	(3)	(2)	(1)	(0)
16.	(4)	(3)	(2)	(1)	(0)	58.	(4)	(3)	(2)	(1)	(0)
17.	(0)	(1)	(2)	(3)	(4)	59.	(4)	(3)	(2)	(1)	(0)
18.	(4)	(3)	(2)	(1)	(0)	60.	(4)	(3)	(2)	(1)	(0)
19.	(0)	(1)	(2)	(3)	(4)	61.	(0)	(1)	(2)	(3)	(4)
20.	(4)	(3)	(2)	(1)	(0)	62.	(0)	(1)	(2)	(3)	(4)
21.	(0)	(1)	(2)	(3)	(4)	63.	(0)	(1)	(2)	(3)	(4)
22.	(4)	(3)	(2)	(1)	(0)	64.	(4)	(3)	(2)	(1)	(0)
23.	(0)	(1)	(2)	(3)	(4)	65.	(4)	(3)	(2)	(1)	(0)
24.	(4)	(3)	(2)	(1)	(0)	66.	(4)	(3)	(2)	(1)	(0)
25.	(4)	(3)	(2)	(1)	(0)	67.	(4)	(3)	(2)	(1)	(0)
26.	(4)	(3)	(2)	(1)	(0)	68.	(0)	(1)	(2)	(3)	(4)
27.	(4)	(3)	(2)	(1)	(0)	69.	(0)	(1)	(2)	(3)	(4)
28.	(4)	(3)	(2)	(1)	(0)	70.	(0)	(1)	(2)	(3)	(4)
29.	(0)	(1)	(2)	(3)	(4)	71.	(4)	(3)	(2)	(1)	(0)
30.	(4)	(3)	(2)	(1)	(0)	72.	(0)	(1)	(2)	(3)	(4)
31.	(0)	(1)	(2)	(3)	(4)	73.	(4)	(3)	(2)	(1)	(0)
32.	(4)	(3)	(2)	(1)	(0)	74.	(4)	(3)	(2)	(1)	(0)
33.	(0)	(1)	(2)	(3)	(4)	75.	(0)	(1)	(2)	(3)	(4)
34.	(0)	(1)	(2)	(3)	(4)	76.	(4)	(3)	(2)	(1)	(0)
35.	(4)	(3)	(2)	(1)	(0)	77.	(0)	(1)	(2)	(3)	(4)
36.	(4)	(3)	(2)	(1)	(0)	78.	(4)	(3)	(2)	(1)	(0)

	STRONGLY AGREE	AGREE	UNDECIDED	DISAGREE	STRONGLY DISAGREE		STRONGLY AGREE	AGREE	UNDECIDED	DISAGREE	STRONGLY DISAGREE
37.	(4)	(3)	(2)	(1)	(0)	79.	(0)	(1)	(2)	(3)	(4)
38.	(4)	(3)	(2)	(1)	(0)	80.	(0)	(1)	(2)	(3)	(4)
39.	(0)	(1)	(2)	(3)	(4)	81.	(4)	(3)	(2)	(1)	(0)
40.	(4)	(3)	(2)	(1)	(0)	82.	(0)	(1)	(2)	(3)	(4)
41.	(4)	(3)	(2)	(1)	(0)	83.	(0)	(1)	(2)	(3)	(4)
42.	(4)	(3)	(2)	(1)	(0)	84.	(4)	(3)	(2)	(1)	(0)

APPENDIX D

Organizational
Ethics
Questionnaire

Instructions

In this questionnaire we are seeking to gather information about the influences that organizations have upon people's lives, with particular emphasis on those influences affecting interpersonal relationships and ethical and moral behavior. In completing this questionnaire, please be as open and candid as possible. If additional space is required, please feel free to add additional pages.

I. Which of the following statements is either True or False for you? Place the letter "T" before each true statement, and the letter "F" before each false statement.

( ) Organizations in our society tend to encourage their members to behave honestly, ethically, caringly, and supportively in their relationships with one another.

( ) Organizations in our society tend to encourage their members to behave unethically, dishonestly, uncaringly, and in nonsupportive ways in their relationships with one another.

( ) Organizations in our society tend to be neutral in relationship to the ethics, honesty, and human interactions of their members.

( ) Organizations in our society tend to pay little attention one way or another to the ethics, honesty, and human interactions of their members unless these in some way influence the success of the organization.

( ) Organizations in our society tend to encourage people to be supportive of one another.

( ) Organizations in our society tend to encourage people to act in terms of their own ethical convictions.

( ) Organizations in our society tend to encourage people to set aside their own ethical convictions when these might interfere with the success of the organization.

II. In what ways, if any, do organizations that you are familiar with (other than your own) encourage people to behave dishonestly, unethically, unfairly, or uncaringly in their relationships with one another? Check the following items that seem to apply and add others as they occur to you.

( ) By pitting people against each other rather than encouraging cooperative relationships

( ) By overemphasizing achievements and bottom-line results (profits and productivity) as opposed to human values

( ) By encouraging people to maintain a distance from one another

( ) By not allowing opportunities for people to get together to know each other

( ) By seeing people as job functions (boss, worker, etc.) rather than as multidimensional human beings

( ) By encouraging people to neglect their own ethical convictions

( ) By encouraging people to overlook or keep quiet about violations of ethics within the organization

III. In what ways, if any, do organizations that you are familiar with (other than your own) encourage people to behave honestly, ethically, fairly, or caringly in their relationships with one another? Check the following items that seem to apply and add others as they occur to you.

( ) By encouraging people to examine the human as well as the economic or achievement consequences of their actions

( ) By developing a positive balance between the people and production aspects of the organization's activities

( ) By providing time and opportunities to get together to know one another as multidimensional human beings

( ) By encouraging people to raise issues with the organization in response to their own ethical concerns and convictions

( ) By encouraging people to be supportive of one another

( ) By encouraging people to develop meaningful relationships with one another

( ) By placing human and ethical concerns at least at the same level as concerns for productivity and achievement

IV. We have listed a number of positive and negative influences on organizational behavior. In this section, we are asking you to provide an account of your own experience. You may or may not wish to include the ideas that were listed in sections II and III. Feel free to use additional pages for your responses if necessary.

A. In what ways, if any, do organizations that you are familiar with, (other than your own) encourage people to behave honestly, ethically, fairly, and caringly in their relationships with one another?

B. In what ways, if any, do organizations that you are familiar with, (other than your own) encourage people to behave dishonestly, unethically, unfairly, and uncaringly in their relationships with one another?

V. In the preceding section you have been asked to summarize your experience with organizations other than your own. In this section we would like to focus on what might be possible within our own organization.

A. What kinds of things could we do or stop doing in our own organization in order to be more constructively supportive of people's efforts to behave ethically, honestly, fairly, and caringly in their relationships with one another?

B. In what ways, if any, does our own organization encourage people to behave dishonestly, unfairly, unethically, and uncaringly in our relationships with one another?

VI. Which types of organizations, if any, that you are familiar with are likely to encourage poor ethics on the part of their members? Check as many or as few as you believe to be appropriate from your experience.

( ) Businesses
( ) Schools
( ) Government agencies
( ) Families
( ) Hospitals
( ) Churches
( ) Professional associations, such as the American Medical Association
( ) Athletic teams
( ) Political parties
( ) Communities

VII. If you have identified organizations as contributing to lack of ethics on the part of their members, check the following factors that you feel might be having a negative influence.

( ) The modeling behavior shown by the leadership
( ) Overemphasis on bottom-line results (profits, productivity, etc.)
( ) The exclusive concern with economics as opposed to human values
( ) Reward structures
( ) Information provided or not provided about ethics, morals, and human relations
( ) The selection process for bringing people into the organization
( ) Promotion practices

(In addition, see the organizational ethics questionnaire in chapter 8.)

APPENDIX E

Lifegain
Health Practices
Norm Indicator

Instructions

The health-related norms that exist in our families, organizations, and communities have a particularly major impact on our health practices. For this reason, this survey is designed to identify some of the key norms that may be influencing our own health-related behavior. The results of this survey can be useful in planning for improvement and change. A norm is what's expected and usual within a group or organization. Norms are really "the way things are," not necessarily the way we would like them to be.

In the questionnaire we have listed a number of the critical norms that have been found to exist in a number of groups in our society. These norms may or may not exist in the groups with which you are associated. We would like you to indicate which of these norms, if any, exist in the groups that you belong to. If you see it as a norm in your group, indicate this by placing an X in the box marked Yes. If none of the groups that you belong to have this as a norm, check the box under No.

In order to see if you have the hang of it, read each of the following statements and then check to see if the answer is the same as the one you would have chosen for your group or organization.

As I see it, it is a norm in one or more of the groups that I belong to...

Yes No
(X) ( ) for people to wear clothes to work
( ) (X) for people to shoot people when they disagree with them

Are the answers the same as the ones you would have given? If they are not, you either belong to some very unusual groups or you should ask for some clarification of this survey.

If your answers are similar and you have no further question, please begin. Keep in mind, all that is needed is your personal opinion. You are not being asked how you think it should be, but rather how you see it.

It is a norm in one or more groups that I belong to:

YES   NO
1. ( ) ( )   for people not to exercise as much as would be healthy for them
2. ( ) ( )   for people to look upon exercise as a grind rather than as a source of pleasure
3. ( ) ( )   for people to use their cars to go short distances even when there is no need to do so
4. ( ) ( )   for people to be surprised when someone uses the stairs instead of the elevator or escalator
5. ( ) ( )   for people to smoke cigarettes, cigars, and pipes to the extent that it is a hazard to their health
6. ( ) ( )   for people to feel that the illness and death statistics regarding smoking will somehow not apply to them
7. ( ) ( )   for smoking to be presented as a desirable behavior in newspaper and magazine ads
8. ( ) ( )   for young people to smoke because it is the thing to do
9. ( ) ( )   for people to take on more responsibility than they can handle
10. ( ) ( )   for people to avoid asking for help if their work load becomes too heavy

11. ( ) ( )   for people not to understand the harmful effects that continued stress can have upon their health

12. ( ) ( )   for people to look upon stress as something that they can't do anything about

13. ( ) ( )   for people to look at being slightly overweight as "natural," particularly among older people

14. ( ) ( )   for people not to balance their food intake with their physical exercise as they grow older

15. ( ) ( )   for people to see children who are slightly overweight as healthier and better cared for than children who aren't

16. ( ) ( )   for people to see desserts such as cake, pie, pudding, and ice cream as an expected part of a lunch or dinner menu

17. ( ) ( )   for parents to encourage children not to leave food on their plates, even if it is more than they want or need

18. ( ) ( )   for people to associate overindulging in food with relaxation, pleasure, and good social relationships

19. ( ) ( )   for people to pay very little attention to the nutritional value of the foods they eat

20. ( ) ( )   for people to have coffee and a roll instead of a nutritious breakfast in the morning

21. ( ) ( )   for people to drink a great many coffee and cola drinks and other caffeine-based beverages

22. ( ) ( )   for the host or hostess at a party to check repeatedly to make sure that everyone's glass is full and that drinks are being continually replenished

23. ( ) ( )   to mention with pride one's own ability or a friend's ability to consume large amounts of alcohol

24. ( ) ( )   to have a drink when one doesn't really want to, just because the others are

25. ( ) ( )   for the use of alcohol to be presented as the "in" thing to do in magazines and TV advertisements

26. ( ) ( )   for young people to be encouraged to drink by their peers

27. ( ) ( )   for waiters and waitresses and others in restaurants to expect that people will be having a drink before or during dinner

28. ( ) ( )   for people to look upon safety rules and regulations as something for others and not themselves to follow

29. ( ) ( )   for people to think it's okay to drive over the posted speed limit so long as they are not caught

30. ( ) ( )   for people not to wear seat belts when they feel it is inconvenient to do so

31. ( ) ( )   for people to drive when drowsy or under the influence of alcohol or medications

YES   NO

32. ( ) ( )   for people to leave pills and other dangerous or poisonous materials around the house in places that might be easily accessible to children

33. ( ) ( )   for people to ignore safety hazards or violations rather than seeing that they are corrected

34. ( ) ( )   for people to keep feelings bottled up inside rather than express them openly

35. ( ) ( )   for people to hold off seeking help with emotional problems until they become very severe

36. ( ) ( )   for people not to handle conflict situations with other people constructively

37. ( ) ( )   for people not to achieve an adequate balance between work, rest, and play in their lives

38. ( ) ( )   for people to bury their creative urges and talents

39. ( ) ( )   for people not to have as much enjoyment in their lives as they are capable of having

40. ( ) ( )   for people to work so hard that they tend to lose contact with other important parts of their lives, for example, their children, their friends, other interests, and so on

A Bibliography
for Cultural Change

GENERAL REFERENCES

ALINSKY, SAUL. *Reveille for Radicals*. New York: Random House, 1969.

BANDURA, ALBERT. *Social Learning Theory*. Englewood Cliffs, N.J.: Prentice-Hall, 1977.

BENNIS, WARREN. *Organization Development: Its Nature, Origins, and Prospects*. Reading, Mass.: Addison-Wesley, 1969.

BLAKE, ROBERT F., and JANE SRYGLEY MOUTON. *The Managerial Grid*. Houston, Tex: Gulf Publishing Co., 1964.

DUBIN, HARRY N. and MO LISS. *Coping Successfully*. New York: Irvington Press, 1981.

FROMM, ERICH. *Escape from Freedom*. New York: Farrar, Straus and Giroux, Inc., 1941.

GALBRAITH, JAY. *Designing Complex Organizations*. Reading, Mass.: Addison-Wesley, 1973.

LASCH, CHRISTOPHER. *The Culture of Narcissism*. New York: W. W. Norton, 1979.

LEWIN, KURT. *Field Theory in Social Science*. New York: Harper and Row, Inc., 1951.

MACCOBY, MICHAEL. *The Gamesman: The New Corporate Leaders*. New York: Simon and Schuster, 1976.

MASLOW, ABRAHAM. *Toward a Psychology of Being*. New York: D. Van Nostrand Co., 1968.

MCGREGOR, DOUGLAS. *The Human Side of Enterprise*. New York: McGraw-Hill, 1960.

NISBET, ROBERT. *The Quest for Community*. New York: Oxford University Press, 1953.

SCHEIN, EDGAR. *Process Consultation: Its Role in Organization Development*. Reading, Mass.: Addison-Wesley, 1969.

REFERENCES ON NORMATIVE SYSTEMS

Books

ALLEN, ROBERT F. *Programs of Personal and Cultural Change*. New York: Appleton-Century-Crofts, 1981. Twelve self-help modules, each dealing with a specific area of health practice. Among these areas are smoking cessation, nutrition, exercise, weight control, and stress management.

ALLEN, ROBERT F., HARRY DUBIN, and SAUL PILNICK. *From Delinquency to Freedom*. New York: Irvington Press, 1981. A detailed account of an award-winning culture-based program for the rehabilitation of delinquent youth. Provides specific guidelines for those wishing to apply guided group interaction and other Normative Systems techniques in programs of individual and cultural change.

ALLEN, ROBERT F., with CHARLOTTE KRAFT. *Beat the System: A Way to Create More Human Environments*. New York: McGraw-Hill, 1980. The most comprehensive book yet published on the subject of Normative Systems. Provides a detailed description of the Normative Systems cultural change process with case illustrations. Suggests ways that individuals and organizations can overcome the tyranny of destructive cultures.

ALLEN, ROBERT F., and CHARLOTTE KRAFT. *The Handbook for Cultural Analysis and Change*. Morristown, N.J.: HRI Press, 1980. This handbook outlines a step-by-step process for planning change programs in groups, organizations, and communities. Illustrations are provided from over 200 different change programs in a variety of settings.

ALLEN, ROBERT F., with SHIRLEY LINDE. *Lifegain: A Culture-Based Approach to Positive Health*. New York: Appleton-Century-Crofts, 1981. This popularly written book helps individuals and groups design their own culture-based programs for positive health. It is currently being used in association with the Healthy America/Lifegain program in communities and organizations throughout the United States.

Films and Audio-visuals

Building the Morristown High School Community. Slide-tape presentation written and produced by Human Resources Institute and the students of Morristown, N.J., High School. Available from HRI Human Resources Institute, Morristown, N.J. by special order only. Introduction to the high school as a culture, stressing people's ability to create the kind of learning environments they'd like to have for themselves.

The Caring Community. Written and produced by Human Resources Institute in cooperation with the State of New Jersey, Department of Human Services, 1978. Available from the New Jersey State Department of Human Services, Trenton, N.J. This New York Film Festival award-winning film deals with the tragic noncaring environments that make up our mental "health" systems. Emphasizes the importance of supportive communities. The film is designed to introduce the HRI Caring Community Program but can also stand alone as a dramatic presentation of the need for community change.

A Child Went Forth... Slide-tape and video presentation written and produced by Human Resources Institute. Available from HRI Human Resources Institute, Morristown, N.J. 1981. Focuses on cultural influences on health practices in today's society.

Lifegain: An Invitation to Positive Health. Slide-tape presentation written and produced by Human Resources Institute in cooperation with Kean College of New Jersey, 1980. Available from HRI Human Resources Institute, Morristown, N.J. Designed to help people review their own health practices and the health norms of the various subcultures to which they belong. Together with the accompanying materials, the program enables participants to work with others in planning and implementing their own life-style changes. Can be used in conjunction with HRI's various Lifegain implementation systems for businesses, schools, families, and communities.

Normative Systems in the Food Industry. Produced by Fred Niles, Inc. in cooperation with the Materials Division of Scientific Resources Inc., 1965. Available from Foodmarketing Institute, Washington, D.C. An award-winning series of four films (approximately two hours in entirety) that provide an instructional program for in-company use. Has been widely used in the food industry and has been the winner of several national instructional film awards. For those concerned with understanding, identifying, and changing cultures in business organizations.

A Place in the Sun. Narrated by Chet Huntley, NBC-TV News, New York, 1972. Available from NBC-TV News or from the Coca-Cola Company, Atlanta, Ga. A news documentary describing a highly successful HRI Normative Systems change program in the Coca-Cola Company's Minute Maid orange groves of central Florida. Highlights gains made by the workers in both productivity and living conditions.

A Place to Begin. Produced by Keep America Beautiful, Inc., New York, 1979. Available from Keep America Beautiful, New York. A film describing the application of the Clean Community System in one of the HRI test cities. The film views the system from the perspective of residents of Macon, Ga., and describes their success in mobilizing a sustained community change program.

Lifegain Articles, Reprints, and Research Reports

ALLEN, ROBERT F. "Assessing Current Health Norms Within Your Organization." Presented at the Southern Regional Health Promotion Planning Conference, Clearwater, Fla. March 13, 1980. A speech concerning the analysis of health norms within organizations.

ALLEN, ROBERT F. "Changing Life-styles Through Changing Organizational Cultures." Presented to the Society of Prospective Medicine, St. Petersburg, Fla., October 1978. An update on the applications of the Lifegain program, a Normative Systems approach to improving health practices. Provides data on levels of perceived organizational and community support.

ALLEN, ROBERT F. "The Corporate Health Buying Spree: Boon or Boondoggle?" *S.A.M. Advanced Management Journal*, 45, no. 2 (Spring 1980), 14–22. An analysis of the problems that arise in corporate health programs and a method to install and sustain successful programs.

ALLEN, ROBERT F. "A Culture-Based Approach to the Improvement of Health Practices." Presented to the Society of Prospective Medicine, San Diego, Calif., October 1977. A discussion of the Normative Systems approach for the improvement of health practices as applied to business organizations, schools, and communities.

ALLEN, ROBERT F. "Designing Wellness Programs." Presented to the Central States Occupational Medical Association Spring Seminar, Chicago, March 9–10, 1979. A description of a culture-based program that can be used by physicians in promoting positive health within corporate settings.

ALLEN, ROBERT F. "A Healthy Community: A Possible Dream." Washington, D.C.: U.S. Department of Health, Education and Welfare, 1979. This booklet recommends the use of community health fairs as an integrative component of a wider community health promotion effort.

ALLEN, ROBERT F. "An Rx for Health." *New York Times*, March 27, 1979, sec. A, p. 25. A recommendation for a culture-based approach to health, suggesting methods for transforming our "national health buying spree" into a national "health revolution."

ALLEN, ROBERT F., HALBE BROWN, MIKE KETCHAM, and LARRY KOSS. *Frost Valley Campers' Kit*. Montclair, N.J.: Frost Valley YMCA, 1979. An administrative guide and counselor's manual that are part of a kit designed to assist camp directors in installing wellness programs in camp settings. The counselor's manual provides specific guidelines.

ALLEN, ROBERT F., RICHARD A. CARLETON, CHARLOTTE KRAFT, and THOMAS LASATER. *Comprehensive Planning for Community Change: A Case Study of the Pawtucket, Rhode Island, Community Heart Health Program*. New York: American Health Foundation, 1980. A description of a culture-based approach to community health describing a National Institute of Health–sponsored longitudinal study of the ability of a community to modify its health practices and its health cultures.

ALLEN, ROBERT F., and CHARLOTTE KRAFT. "Building Wellness Cultures on a Community Level." Selected Papers Series, Morristown, N.J.: HRI Press, 1979. This reprint in HRI's

Selected Papers Series describes ways in which communities can apply the Lifegain Healthy Community System.

ALLEN, ROBERT F., and CHARLOTTE KRAFT. "Changing Our Health Cultures: A Family Guide to Wellness and Positive Health." *Parents Magazine*, July 1980, pp. 61–65. This reprint suggests ways in which people can come together within the family unit to build positive health cultures that are supportive of the changes they wish to make in their lives.

ALLEN, ROBERT F., and CHARLOTTE KRAFT. "You Can Mobilize Communities Toward Health." *Perspective Journal* (Journal of the Association of Professional YMCA Directors) 6, nos. 2 and 3 (Winter and Spring 1980). A description of a program through which YMCA leaders throughout the country might organize their communities toward better health.

ALLEN, ROBERT F., and DEBORAH STAR. "Operation Lifegain: A Program of Health Promotion on a Community Level." Presented to the Conference on Corporate Commitment to Health, June 9–10, 1980, Washington, D.C. This paper describes a recommended national program for assisting communities and promoting positive health.

DRURY, BARBARA, and ROBERT F. ALLEN. "Maximizing Employee Health by Changing the Corporate Culture." Presented to the American Public Health Association, Washington, D.C., November 1977. A description of the Normative Systems program to improve employee health through the Lifegain program.

Other Normative Systems Applications— Articles, Reprints, and Research Reports

ALLEN, ROBERT F. "The Ik in the Office." *Organizational Dynamics*, Winter 1980, pp. 26–41. A discussion of cultural impact on personal values.

ALLEN, ROBERT F. "Increasing Group Effectiveness Through Normative Systems." Morristown, N.J.: HRI Press, 1975. This article focuses on ways of increasing small-group effectiveness through the Normative Systems process.

ALLEN, ROBERT F. "Keine Rolle fur Unbeteiligte." *Gruppendynamik*, no. 3, July 1970. This brief article suggests some ways in which behavioral scientists might be more helpful to social change movements.

ALLEN, ROBERT F. "Motivation Through Normative Systems." *Journal of Duttweiler Institute*, Zurich, Switz., no. 3, March 1972. This paper, presented to the Duttweiler Institute in 1971, suggests an approach to motivation in organizations through the application of cultural change programs.

ALLEN, ROBERT F. "Normative Systems: An Approach to Increasing Organizational Effectiveness." Morristown, N.J.: Scientific Resources Institute (SRI) Press, 1970. A paper describing the Normative Systems process as it applies to increasing organizational effectiveness.

ALLEN, ROBERT F. "Normative Systems Programs in Union Organizations." Morristown, N.J.: HRI Press, 1975. This is a paper describing an approach to installing Normative Systems programs in union organizations.

ALLEN, ROBERT F. "When Are Results Not Results?" Selected Papers Series of the American Society for Training and Development, March 1979. A discussion of why short-term results of change efforts don't last and how this can be remedied.

ALLEN, ROBERT F., et al. *The Caring Community*. Morristown, N.J.: HRI Press, 1978. A series of instruments designed to aid those in the mental health field to improve patient services.

ALLEN, ROBERT F., et al. "The Normative Systems Orientation Program." Morristown, N.J.: HRI Press, 1975. This orientation program was prepared for use in the supermarket industry and published by the Quaker Oats Company in association with the Super Market Institute.

ALLEN, ROBERT F., and FRANK DYER. "A Tool for Tapping the Organizational Unconscious." *Personnel Journal*, March 1980, pp. 192–98. A description and discussion of instruments for use in culture change programs.

ALLEN, ROBERT F., and MICHAEL HIGGINS. "The Absenteeism Culture: Becoming Attendance Oriented." *Personnel*, January 1979, pp. 192–99. A description of a cultural approach to the improvement of attendance in companies.

ALLEN, ROBERT F., and CHARLOTTE KRAFT. "From Burn–out to Turn–on: Improving the Quality of Hospital Work Life." *Hospital Forum* (Journal of the Association of Western Hospitals), Spring 1981, pp. 18–28. A cultural approach to improving the quality of work life for nurses, doctors, and other hospital workers.

ALLEN, ROBERT F., and RICHARD MURPHY. "Getting Started: The Development of a New Company." *Business* 29, no. 4 (July–August 1979), 26–34. Describes the process by which a group of people started a new division of Hoffmann–LaRoche in Puerto Rico.

ALLEN, ROBERT F., and SAUL PILNICK, "Confronting the Shadow Organization: How to Detect and Defeat Negative Norms." *Organizational Dynamics* (Journal of the American Management Association), Spring 1973. A discussion of the impact of norms on the overall functioning of an organization.

ALLEN, ROBERT F., and SAUL PILNICK. "Guided Group Interaction." *Encyclopedia of Social Work*. New York: American Association of Social Work, 1974. Describes the Guided Group Interaction process, particularly as it applies in social work settings.

ALLEN, ROBERT F., and SAUL PILNICK, "Report on Normative Systems in European Business Organizations." Morristown, N.J.: Materials Division of Scientific Resources Inc., 1970. This report describes a study, conducted by the authors, of normative cultures in European business organizations and suggests approaches to increasing organizational effectiveness. The report resulted in a series of seminars conducted for presidents of European organizations.

ALLEN, ROBERT F., with SAUL PILNICK, et al. "The Peer Group in Adolescence." State of New York, Division of Youth, 1968. This pamphlet describes the role of a peer group in adolescence with ways in which organizations and communities can be supportive of positive peer group influence.

ALLEN, ROBERT F., SAUL PILNICK, and COLIN PARK. "The Accounting Executive's Shadow Organization." *Management Accounting* (Journal of the National Association of Accountants) 4, no. 7 (January 1974), 11–14. A discussion of the impact of norms on accounting effectiveness.

ALLEN, ROBERT F., SAUL PILNICK, and STANLEY SILVERZWEIG. "Conflict Resolution—Team Building for Police and Ghetto Residents." Presented to symposium of the American Psychological Association, San Francisco, 1968. A research paper on the application of Normative Systems theory to the building of effective team relationships between urban ghetto residents and police officers.

ALLEN, ROBERT F., with J. ROSNER. "Social Integration and the English Language Development of Puerto Rican Children." New York: Ford Foundation, 1954. A study of the impact of peer cultures on English language development of Puerto Rican children conducted in New York City.

ALLEN, ROBERT F., and STANLEY SILVERZWEIG. "Group Norms: Their Influence on Training Effectiveness." *Handbook of Training and Development*. Madison, Wis.: American Society for Training and Development, 1975. An analysis of the role of culture in the orientation, training, and development of group and organizational members.

ALLEN, ROBERT F., and STANLEY SILVERZWEIG. *Proper Price Marking*. Morristown, N.J.: SRI Press, 1969. A system to help supermarkets build positive norms in the area of price marking.

ALLEN, ROBERT F., STANLEY SILVERZWEIG, et al.,*Employment of the Disadvantaged*. Chicago: Super Market Institute, 1968. A booklet providing effective guidelines for changing negative norms related to the selection and allocation of human resources in the supermarket industry.

ALLEN, ROBERT F., STANLEY SILVERZWEIG, and SAUL PILNICK. *Customer Courtesy*. Chicago: Super Market Institute, 1967. A system to help supermarkets build positive norms in the area of customer relations.

ALLEN, ROBERT F., STANLEY SILVERZWEIG, and MARILYN SCHNEIDER. *Changing Our Litter Culture: Normative Systems Action Research Model for the Reduction of Litter in American Communities*. New York: Keep America Beautiful, Inc., 1974. A report on the successful application of Normative Systems to the problem of litter and littering behavior.

ALLEN, ROBERT F., and JOHN WAGNER. *Current Good Manufacturing Practices*. Morristown, N.J.: HRI Press, 1978. A series of manuals for implementing Current Good Manufacturing Practices Programs in pharmaceutical companies.

"ALP–Update." *Foodline*. Winter Haven, Fla.: The Coca-Cola Company Foods Division, January–February, 1971, pp. 3–5. A description of the Agricultural Labor Project, the application of Normative Systems to improving the work and living styles of Florida citrus workers.

"A 'Behavior Business' Is Born." *Food Topics* (a magazine for supermarket management), January 1967, pp. 17–21. A description of SRI's early work to apply Normative Systems methodology to the problem of the retail food trade.

BLANK, JOSEPH P. "Migrants No More." *Reader's Digest*, July 1975, pp. 98–102. A dramatic description of the change in lives of the Florida citrus grove workers who participated in a Normative Systems cultural change program.

"An Experiment in Problem Solving Through Personnel Involvement." *Chain Store Age*, May 1970. A description of a Normative Systems program designed to involve store-level supermarket employees in changing their negative norms in key areas of supermarket functioning.

GARNER, PHIL. "A New Life for Migrant Workers." *Atlanta Journal and Constitution Magazine*, January 23, 1972, pp. 8–14. This article describes a successful Normative Systems program with migrant workers in central Florida.

"How to Reach Labor's Silent Majority." Industrial Bulletin. New York State Department of Labor, March 1970. A description of a Normative Systems program for trade union leaders.

KNEBEL, FLETCHER. "The White Cop and the Black Rebel." *Look*, February 6, 1968, pp. 18–21. A description of a program designed to change norms affecting the relationship between a white policeman and a black ghetto resident.

KRAFT, CHARLOTTE. "Changing Our Litter Culture." HRI Selected Paper Series, 1979. Story of a three-city pilot program to reduce litter using the Normative Systems cultural change process.

LARKIN, TIMOTHY. "Adios to Migrancy." *Manpower* (Journal of the United States Department of Labor), August 1974, pp. 15–22. A comprehensive review of the results achieved through the application of Normative Systems to the problems of migrancy in central Florida.

"Negro Arrests Cop: Role-Switching Games Aim at Ghetto Peace." *Wall Street Journal*, Midwest Edition, August 2, 1968. A news report on the Grand Rapids, Michigan, project aimed at building positive-interaction norms between police and ghetto residents.

POLSKY, HOWARD. *Cottage Six: The Social System of Delinquent Boys in Residential Treatment*. New York: Russell Sage, 1962. A pioneer study of the cultural influences on rehabilitation in a delinquency treatment institution.

A Project in Progress. Atlanta, Ga.: The Coca-Cola Company, May 1973–September 1974. A series of status reports on the Agricultural Labor Project in central Florida, describing the components of the project, its guiding principles, and its early results.

SILVERZWEIG, STANLEY, and ROBERT F. ALLEN. "Changing the Corporate Culture." *Sloan Management Review* (Journal of the Alfred P. Sloan School of Management), Cambridge, Mass.: Massachusetts Institute of Technology, Spring 1976, pp. 33–49. A comprehensive introduction to Normative Systems theory and application, tracing the progress by which seven American businesses learned to modify their cultures and achieve dramatic results.

SILVERZWEIG, STANLEY, and ROBERT F. ALLEN, et al. *Employment of the Disadvantaged*. Chicago: Super Market Institute, 1968. A booklet providing effective guidelines for changing negative norms related to the selection and allocation of human resources in the supermarket industry.

SILVERZWEIG, STANLEY, ROBERT F. ALLEN, and SAUL PILNICK, et al. *The SRI Organic Reading and Writing Laboratory*. Morristown, N.J.: SRI Press, 1966. A program to improve learning norms in the area of language development.

SILVERZWEIG, STANLEY, ROBERT F. ALLEN, and SAUL PILNICK, et al. *Teacher Aide Training System*. New York: Macmillan, 1968. A comprehensive training program directed toward preparing educational systems for the effective use of teacher auxiliaries.

Index

227